THE CHRISTIAN LIFE

A NAZARENE PERSPECTIVE

Carla D. Sunberg

NAZARENE PUBLISHING HOUSE
Kansas City, Missouri, USA

Copyright © 2025 by Carla D. Sunberg
Nazarene Publishing House
PO Box 419527
Kansas City, MO 64141

Published in cooperation with the Board of General Superintendents for the Church of the Nazarene.

978-0-8341-4337-1

All rights reserved. No part of this publication may be reproduced, stored in a retrieval system, or transmitted in any form or by any means—for example, electronic, photocopy, recording—without the prior written permission of the publisher. The only exception is brief quotations in printed reviews.

Cover Design: Caines Design
Interior Design: Sharon Page

All Scripture quotations, unless indicated, are taken from THE HOLY BIBLE, NEW INTERNATIONAL VERSION®, NIV®. Copyright © 1973, 1978, 1984, 2011 by Biblica, Inc.® Used by permission. All rights reserved worldwide.

Scriptures marked (NRSVUE) are from the New Revised Standard Version, Updated Edition (NRSVUE). Copyright © 2021 National Council of Churches of Christ in the United States of America. Used by permission. All rights reserved worldwide.

Scriptures marked (RSV) are from the *Revised Standard Version* (RSV) of the Bible, copyright 1946, 1952, 1971 by the Division of Christian Education of the national Council of the Churches of Christ in the USA. Used by permission.

The internet addresses, email addresses, and phone numbers in this book are accurate at the time of publication. They are provided as a resource. Nazarene Publishing House does not endorse them or vouch for their content or permanence.

CONTENTS

Foreword by Dr. David A. Busic   5
Introduction (¶28–28.2)   7

Section I: We Are Called To . . .
1. Discipleship within the Family of God (¶28.3)   33
2. Engage in Reconciling Love (¶28.4)   43
3. Consecrate Our Time to God (¶28.5)   57
4. Value Learning (¶28.6)   63
5. Offer Our Work in Sacrifice to God (¶28.7)   71
6. Careful and Considered Use of Media and Technology (¶28.8)   77
7. Care for Creation (¶28.9)   83
8. Be Peacemakers (¶28.10)   89

Section II: We Are Called From . . .
9. Things That Hinder Us (¶29)   99
10. Subversive Entertainments and Activities (¶29.1)   103
11. Unhealthy Habits (¶29.2)   113
12. Alcohol and Other Intoxicating Substances (¶29.3–29.4)   121
13. Greed (¶29.5)   137
14. Attitudes and Actions That Devalue Others (¶29.6)   143
15. Loyalties That Compete with Christ's Lordship (¶29.7)   147
16. Corruption (¶29.8)   153

Conclusion   159

FOREWORD

With the Bible as our supreme guide, illuminated by the Holy Spirit, the Church of the Nazarene *Manual* exists as our official, agreed-upon statement of faith, practice, and polity. Within the *Manual* is the Covenant of Christian Conduct, designed to help Nazarenes around the world navigate some of the vital issues in contemporary society.

The Board of General Superintendents understands that cultural dynamics can be difficult to navigate. We receive many requests for resources to help pastors and leaders add context and clarity to the questions and conversations happening in their local churches. To that end, the Board of General Superintendents asked our colleague Dr. Carla Sunberg to write *The Christian Life: A Nazarene Perspective*.

In the following pages, Dr. Sunberg explores the implications of our *Manual* statement on what it means to live a holy life in a complex world. Our prayer is that this book will lead you into a deeper and more beautiful understanding of God's call on every believer to live Christlike lives that bear witness to the gospel of Jesus Christ and bring glory to God.

Dr. David Busic
Chair, Board of General Superintendents
February 2025

INTRODUCTION (¶28–28.2)

The mission statement of the Church of the Nazarene is "to make Christlike disciples in the nations." Unpacking that statement comes with an invitation to a journey in which we turn from the ways of this world and begin moving in a direction where we become more and more like Christ.[1]

In the early centuries of Christianity, a leader named Origen challenged believers to participate in the life of Christ, which he described as a spiritual journey using the metaphor of a mirror (see 2 Cor. 3:18, NRSVUE). He said to imagine that each of us was created with a mirror in which we were to reflect the image of God, which is Christ. When Adam and Eve sinned, they turned their backs on God and the *reflection* was lost, but the beauty and love of God are revealed when we discover that the *mirror* was not lost. The capacity of humankind to reflect the image of God has always remained within creation.[2] Because of the life of Christ, we are able to repent, turn

---

1. For greater detail and understanding about the journey of discipleship, see David A. Busic, *Way, Truth, Life: Discipleship as a Journey of Grace* (Kansas City, MO: The Foundry Publishing, 2021).

2. See Luke 15:8–10. The early church fathers saw the parable of the lost coin as representing the image, which was *lost* in the home but nevertheless was still always *in* the home. The image of God can always be restored.

INTRODUCTION

back around, and once again find ourselves in a face-to-face relationship with God. The restorative work of God returns humanity to the original relationship with God through Jesus.

As we begin this restored relationship with Jesus, we discover that we are on a journey in which we are drawn ever closer to him. To press Origen's original illustration a little, we might also consider the fact that the mirror has been smudged or may even be a little dirty from the journey of life. Therefore, the reflection may not be entirely clear. There is a moment in which the mirror needs to be cleansed so the reflection of Christ becomes perfect, without blemish.[3] We call this process entire sanctification, and it is an invitation to a deeper walk with Jesus Christ that can only happen through the synergizing of our entire consecration with the work of the Holy Spirit. This is the call to holiness.

When we use a mirror, we may notice that the closer we are to the mirror, the more the reflection fills it up. In this journey toward Christlikeness, the closer we draw to Christ, the more we reflect Christ in all we do. The goal is for our mirror to be so filled with Christ that someone looking in our direction can't tell if they are seeing us, or Christ, because of the holiness of Christ reflected in us. We do not make ourselves holy, nor are we ourselves holy; rather, participation in the holiness of Jesus can permeate our lives.

Along the entire journey, we live in response to Christ. The early church fathers would tell us that, if we want to become like Christ, we need to *practice* becoming like him. Many young people are inspired by the star athletes of the day, so

---

3. A larger discussion on an understanding of perfection can be found in chapter 11.

much so that practicing and imitating their skills may become a daily habit because this is the way to become like someone we admire. The same is true for those seeking Christlikeness, and early church leaders called it the practice of virtue—that is, intentionally adopting the practices of Christ on a daily basis while on the journey toward Christlikeness. The practice of virtue is the work of God and humankind together, but it is not a works-based salvation. We do not try to become like Christ in order to be saved, for salvation is a free gift from God; however, we are called to a lifelong journey of participating in the life of Christ, transformed by his holiness. The call to holiness, and the presence of the Holy Spirit in our lives, draws us into God's restorative work. That is Christlike discipleship.

The Church of the Nazarene challenges every believer to continue the journey toward Christlikeness. We should never become satisfied or complacent about where we are on that journey. Paul lays this out for us in Philippians 3:12-14: "Not that I have already obtained all this, or have already arrived at my goal, but I press on to take hold of that for which Christ Jesus took hold of me. Brothers and sisters, I do not consider myself yet to have taken hold of it. But one thing I do: Forgetting what is behind and straining toward what is ahead, I press on toward the goal to win the prize for which God has called me heavenward in Christ Jesus." We press on toward the goal, and Jesus is that goal.

Discussions of the Christian life have been ongoing in the Church of the Nazarene for decades. The message of holiness, or Christlikeness, is foundational to our understanding of the Christian life, and that is why our founders felt it was important to include this section in the Church of the Nazarene *Manual*. New editions of the *Manual* are published and reissued

INTRODUCTION

in correlation with the denomination's quadrennial General Assembly.[4] The *Manual* constitutes the denomination's "official agreed-upon statement of faith, practice, and polity."[5] The 2023 edition of the *Manual* contains eleven principal sections called Parts. Part III is The Covenant of Christian Conduct, which includes seven subheadings: "The Christian Life," "Sanctity of Human Life," "Human Sexuality and Marriage," "Christian Stewardship," "Church Officers," "Rules of Order," and "Amending the Covenant of Christian Conduct." The goal of this book is to take a deeper look at the section "The Christian Life," but this book in no way replaces or supersedes what is written in the *Manual*.

Interestingly, this particular section of the *Manual* was not always known as The Covenant of Christian Conduct. This name is a fairly recent occurrence in Nazarene history. Prior to 2001, Part III of the *Manual* was known as the Special Rules. The Special Rules (and subsequent Covenant of Christian Conduct) was intended to parallel the section of the 1898 *Manual* of Phineas F. Bresee's Church of the Nazarene entitled Special Advices.[6] That section included statements on "Temperance," "Tobacco," "Christian Giving," "Marriage," "Divorce," "Baptism," "Mode,"[7] "Re-Baptism," "Foreign Missions," and

---

4. The term "quadrennial General Assembly" refers to the Church of the Nazarene's practice of gathering elected and appointed delegates and other denominational leaders in a formal conference every four years.

5. Church of the Nazarene, *Manual: 2023* (Kansas City, MO: Nazarene Publishing House, 2023), 7.

6. W. T. Purkiser, *Called unto Holiness, Volume Two: The Story of the Nazarenes; The Second Twenty-Five Years, 1933–58* (Kansas City, MO: Beacon Hill Press of Kansas City, 1983), 63.

7. The term "mode" refers to the different ways an individual can be baptized.

"Christian Testimony."[8] The denomination has always placed importance on the way Nazarenes live out our lives in the world. Special Advices remained through the first six editions of the *Manual*, from 1907 through 1923. The title was changed to Special Rules in the 1928 edition, although we cannot find documentation to indicate why the change was made.

In 2001, Special Rules was renamed The Covenant of Christian Conduct by action of the Twenty-Fifth General Assembly of the Church of the Nazarene in Indianapolis, Indiana, USA. Assembly documentation helps us understand the heart of the denomination in making this change. The theological and spiritual father of the Holiness Movement was John Wesley, an eighteenth-century Englishman who earnestly sought holiness of heart and life, both for himself and for his fellow believers. He and his brother, Charles, began a movement that impacted the whole world—Methodism. The Church of the Nazarene has roots in both the Methodist Church and the American Holiness Movement of the nineteenth century. If Wesley is our father, then the American Holiness Movement is our mother, and we were birthed in this union. By the twenty-first century, the eighteenth-century Wesleyan term "rules" no longer carried the same connotation in society but was seen in negative terms. The term "covenant" was adopted specifically because it was a biblical term, carrying with it the understanding of a solemn promise of great meaning—a vow to be kept sacred and pure. The term also possesses the advantage of analogy to other

---

8. Church of the Nazarene, *Manual: 1898* (Los Angeles, 1898), 19–24. This same edition of the *Manual* contains another section called Special Rules that deals only with polity issues and ministry roles. The section Special Advices offers more parallels to the section of the current edition of the *Manual* called The Covenant of Christian Conduct.

covenant relationships, such as marriage, thus communicating the original and ongoing intent more effectively. Covenant also carries the responsibility of the community of faith to nurture the individual believer in holiness, as well as the responsibility of individual believers to honor the character of Christian community through holy living.

As part of the Church of the Nazarene, you are invited into this covenant relationship in which the church has responsibility to nurture you in the faith and you have the opportunity to partner in your own spiritual growth and development. The transformational work of the Holy Spirit means that a person is changed; we do not need to remain as we once were. This work on "The Christian Life" is an invitation into a relationship of transformation in Christ that includes a covenant with a community of faith that leads to an understanding of what Christlikeness may look like in this world.

The sections that you find bolded and numbered are paragraphs taken directly from the 2023 edition of the *Manual*, together with their supporting Scripture references. It is our desire to unpack both the *Manual* paragraphs (**bold**) and the accompanying scriptures (*italics*) as an encouragement to participate in the holiness journey and in the life of Christ.

A. The Christian Life

◆ **28. The church joyfully proclaims the good news that new life can be found through Jesus Christ. Scripture begins with God's good work of creating, though the appearance and ever-increasingly devastating effects of sin followed. Yet, because of God's grace and mercy, God constantly acts to restore what has been damaged by sin. The fullness of God's redemptive plan is revealed in the good news of the gospel that in Christ God was reconciling the world to himself. "If anyone is in Christ, the new creation has**

come: the old has gone, the new is here!" (2 Corinthians 5:17–19). God's restorative work calls the people of God to embody and witness to this new life in the present day. The Christian life calls the disciple, the whole person—body, mind, and spirit—to commitments and choices in response to God's transforming grace. Therefore, "offer your bodies as a living sacrifice, holy and pleasing to God—this is your true and proper worship. Do not conform to the pattern of this world, but be transformed by the renewing of your mind" (Romans 12:1b–2a).
(Rom. 12:1–2; Eph. 4:22–24; Col. 3:9–11; 1 Thess. 5:23–24)

2 Corinthians 5:17–19

Therefore, if anyone is in Christ, the new creation has come: The old has gone, the new is here! All this is from God, who reconciled us to himself through Christ and gave us the ministry of reconciliation: that God was reconciling the world to himself in Christ, not counting people's sins against them. And he has committed to us the message of reconciliation.

The church does indeed proclaim the good news that, when we are in Christ, we are restored in our relationship to God and to others. Jesus is the master reconciler. The gulf between God and humanity grew wide as a result of sin, and no matter how hard we as humans might have tried, we simply could not make our way back to God on a consistent basis. Enter Jesus. His death on the cross brought about the reconciliation of a relationship that was damaged by humanity, not by God. We, the humans, needed assistance getting back to God, and "God was reconciling the world to himself in Christ."

Because of God's great love for us, God came to earth in human flesh just to create a pathway for reconciliation. This pathway allows for the old to be gone and the new to come through holy love, resulting in reconciliation. Reconciliation also leads to restoration in us of the image of God. This was God's plan and desire for all of humanity—to walk and talk with him in a face-to-face relationship on a daily basis. Amazingly, once we become partakers of this reconciliation, we too become part of the process of reconciliation. We are to become God's ambassadors, working to reconcile other relationships. God is making his appeal through us to a hurting world.

If we are to be ambassadors of reconciliation as we continue to grow in grace, God may reveal to us that we have damaged relationships that need healing. Humanity's relationship to God, as well as humanity's relationship to itself, was derailed through sin. Jesus came to remind us that the Law was summed up in the simple truth that we are to love God and love neighbor. The Christian life takes into account these relationships and the responsibility of serving as an ambassador of reconciliation. The challenge to following after Christ and becoming a Christlike disciple is great because it is not all about us; it is also about the lives of others around us who may just need to see Christ in us.

Romans 12:1-2

Therefore, I urge you, brothers and sisters, in view of God's mercy, to offer your bodies as a living sacrifice, holy and pleasing to God—this is your true and proper worship. Do not conform to the pattern of this world, but be transformed by the renewing of your mind. Then you will be able to test and approve what God's will is—his good, pleasing and perfect will.

Introduction

The invitation to the Christian life is not to be taken lightly. Twentieth-century German pastor and theologian Dietrich Bonhoeffer offered a contrast between cheap and costly grace. "Cheap grace," he said, "means the justification of sin without the justification of the sinner."[9] He continued, "Cheap grace is the preaching of forgiveness without requiring repentance, baptism without church discipline. . . . Cheap grace is grace without discipleship, grace without the cross, grace without Jesus Christ, living and incarnate."[10] Bonhoeffer compared cheap grace to costly grace, which is "the treasure hidden in the field; for the sake of it a man will gladly go and sell all that he has. It is the pearl of great price to buy for which the merchant will sell all his goods. It is the kingly rule of Christ, for whose sake a man will pluck out the eye which causes him to stumble; it is the call of Jesus Christ at which the disciple leaves his nets and follows him."[11]

The apostle Paul asks us literally to offer ourselves as a living sacrifice to God. The first-century Roman world had a very particular understanding of sacrifice, located within a culture that was thoroughly embraced by the whole of society. Worship of the gods was a way of life, and participation in that worship was considered a reflection of one's citizenship. Paul's call to the Christians of Rome was radical, and this sacrifice was profoundly different from that of pagan worship, where the sacrifice was dead. Our sacrifice is to be living, holy, and acceptable, which means it is also holistic, encompassing every facet of our lives.

---

9. Dietrich Bonhoeffer, *The Cost of Discipleship* (New York: Touchstone, 1995), 43.
10. Bonhoeffer, *The Cost of Discipleship*, 44–45.
11. Bonhoeffer, *The Cost of Discipleship*, 45.

INTRODUCTION

What matters most in the life of the believer is the work of the Holy Spirit as the agent of change. "To be conformed is to fit comfortably within the present age. To be transformed is to be fitted by God for the age to come. Consequently, Christians are often misfits in the world's eyes."[12] This is where we don't always feel comfortable. Who wants to be a misfit? The pull of culture and society has always been great, and that is why this radical transformation through the presence of the Spirit is so astonishing. Christianity isn't just a head game; it is a full-body consecration. As such, "the bodily obedience of Christians was for Paul the essential expression of worship to God the Creator in the world of everyday."[13]

Far too often, we try to separate our "secular" and "religious" lives. Paul would never have recognized this type of discipleship because the whole of the person is transformed, even in this lifetime. When we lean into the secular-religious dichotomy, we begin to embrace cheap grace. Bonhoeffer offered this warning to German church and society in the middle of the twentieth century:

> But do we also realize that this cheap grace has turned back upon us like a boomerang? The price we are having to pay today in the shape of the collapse of the organized Church is only the inevitable consequence of our policy of making grace available to all at too low a cost. We gave away the word and sacraments wholesale, we baptized, confirmed, and absolved a whole nation unasked and without condition. Our humanitarian sentiment made us

---

12. William M. Greathouse and George Lyons, *Romans 9-16: A Commentary in the Wesleyan Tradition*, New Beacon Bible Commentary (Kansas City, MO: Beacon Hill Press of Kansas City, 2008), Kindle Location 3070.

13. Greathouse and Lyons, *Romans 9–16*, Kindle Location 3155.

Introduction

give that which was holy to the scornful and unbelieving. We poured forth unending streams of grace. But the call to follow Jesus in the narrow way was hardly ever heard.[14] The call of the Christian life is to follow Jesus in the narrow way. The problem is that living sacrifices can crawl off the altar! We can't climb up on the altar on Sunday morning and spend the rest of the week somewhere else. This is a journey of life-long transformation that requires placing ourselves on the altar on a daily basis.

Ephesians 4:22–24

You were taught, with regard to your former way of life, to put off your old self, which is being corrupted by its deceitful desires; to be made new in the attitude of your minds; and to put on the new self, created to be like God in true righteousness and holiness.

Discipleship has always had a central place in the Christian life. The apostle Paul assumed that the new believers in Ephesus had been taught what it meant to be a disciple of Jesus Christ. Within the new Christian church, there were those who had been raised in the Jewish faith and would have had a moral framework within which they lived their lives. The pagans worshiped numerous gods and engaged in sexual practice as part of that worship. Pagans were encouraged by society to satisfy every longing and desire, without boundary. What we find in Ephesus is an embrace of the pagan lifestyle and the encouragement to normalize first-century culture. Paul is rather emphatic when he declares, "This is not how you came to know Christ!" (see vv. 20–21).

---

14. Bonhoeffer, *The Cost of Discipleship*, 54.

INTRODUCTION

When one puts on Christ, there is the expectation of a lifestyle change. The old is gone, and behold! Everything becomes new. Paul was not saying this is easy, but it is the expectation. At the same time, we shouldn't miss the good news here. No one says we are to do this all on our own. There are two factors to consider. The first is that we are empowered by putting on Christ. We become partakers of the divine nature, and in doing so, we put on Christ's holiness. This is not our own holiness but Christ living in us, who empowers us to live a new life. Second, the church is to be a community of faith that is countercultural, becoming an incubator for those growing in righteousness and holiness. In other words, we are to encourage one another in this new life.

Colossians 3:9–11

Do not lie to each other, since you have taken off your old self with its practices and have put on the new self, which is being renewed in knowledge in the image of its Creator. Here there is no Gentile or Jew, circumcised or uncircumcised, barbarian, Scythian, slave or free, but Christ is all, and is in all.

In writing to the church in Colossae, Paul speaks again to those who are being discipled. They have already been made new, saved, and sanctified. The old is gone, and the new has now come. At the same time, the community of believers must take this life of discipleship seriously, speaking truth to one another and encouraging each other to live into the new self. John Chrysostom, a well-known church father, preached in the late fourth and early fifth centuries. He gave us this illustration regarding Paul's comments:

> Does Paul write as though these things were in us? There is no contradiction. It is similar to one who has scoured a statue that was filthy, recast it, and displayed it new and bright, explaining that the rust was eaten off and destroyed. Yet he recommends diligence in clearing away the future rust. He does not contradict himself, for it is not that rust which he scoured off that he recommends should be cleared away but that which grew afterwards. So it is not that former putting to death he speaks of here, nor those fornications, but those which afterward grow.[15]

We are like a statue that has been cleaned but must now work to remain clean, for we have been renewed. This renewal means that all external distinctions—such as ethnicity, class, race, and gender—have been removed. We no longer brag about who we are in the flesh but about who we are in Christ. Jesus Christ is our all in all. He becomes the defining point of our lives. The renewed image, or statue, is in the image of Christ.

Examining Chrysostom's illustration of the statue, we realize that there is some elbow grease required to keep the statue clean. It's not just cleaned once then magically remains that way. I think we'd like to see that happen in our spiritual lives, but it's not realistic. Yes, we believe in the cleansing power of God's Holy Spirit to make us renewed in the image of God. That is a beautiful thing, but it is just the beginning of an exciting journey in which we find renewal day after day. Temptations of the past may still surround us, and we have to learn how, in the power of the Spirit, to put aside the past (see 1 Cor. 9:26–27). We have to learn that Jesus can be our all in all.

---

15. John Chrysostom, *Homilies on Colossians*, 8.

INTRODUCTION

1 Thessalonians 5:23–24

May God himself, the God of peace, sanctify you through and through. May your whole spirit, soul and body be kept blameless at the coming of our Lord Jesus Christ. The one who calls you is faithful, and he will do it.

Jesus is our all in all because he sanctifies us "through and through." This passage is one we use often in our Wesleyan-Holiness tradition because it points to entire sanctification. Even so, there have been times when it has been misunderstood. Embracing this second work of grace, subsequent to salvation, is important in the life of the believer. The danger is in thinking that, once the crisis point has been experienced, then the journey has come to an end.

Dr. Ralph Earle, who was a professor of New Testament at Nazarene Theological Seminary and a member of the Bible translation team for the New International Version, told us to look at the Luther Bible where this passage is translated into German as, "*heilige euch durch und durch.*" In English this would read, "make you (all) holy through and through." This scripture is a call for the entire community of faith to be sanctified. Dr. Earle reiterated the idea of "through and through," and the importance of understanding the depth of this activity—not just on a shallow level but through, and through, and through—until every part of our being is made clean by the power of the Holy Spirit.[16] Our intentions can be made clean, through and through. The Russian translation of this passage uses an

---

16. These are the author's personal memories of being a teenager at Kansas City First Church of the Nazarene and hearing Dr. Ralph Earle preach. It is a great reminder that sometimes a bit of a sermon may stay with you for a lifetime.

imperfect verb, leaving the reader with an understanding of an ongoing and continuous activity that has not yet reached completion.[17] We are to be sanctified, or made holy, every day of our lives until we have reached the goal—to be God's holy people.

Although we encourage every believer to experience entire sanctification, we then also embrace sanctification as an ongoing activity that continues throughout the remainder of life because our spirit, soul, and body are constantly changing. Who you were yesterday may not be the same person you are today. Relationally, we are not the same because there are constantly new people coming into and out of our lives. In terms of our reactions, we are not who we were yesterday because every day we are confronted with new situations and new opportunities to which to respond.

Therefore, Paul's prayer is the prayer we all need—that we would be sanctified through and through; yes, yesterday, but even more so today, and tomorrow, and the days to come. We pray that our sanctification will continue on to completion—meaning it will continue all the way through life until, eventually, we are able to stand sound and blameless before our Lord. This is the good news of restoration, as well as the bold invitation into a new way of living and relating to God and others. Come, let's follow Jesus into this truth.

◆ 28.1. God's people commit themselves to enduring scriptural truth, found in both the Old and New Testaments. We hold that the Ten Commandments, as reaffirmed in the teachings of Jesus Christ, demonstrated in the Great Commandment and the Sermon

---

17. The author's heart languages include German and Russian, which has brought a fuller understanding to some biblical passages.

on the Mount constitute the basic Christian ethic. We consider it imperative that in every specific cultural context we earnestly seek the guidance of the Holy Spirit, and the wisdom of the Christian tradition in living Christlike lives.
(John 14:26; 16:13)

When one of the disciples was struggling to find his way, Jesus answered, "I am the way and the truth and the life. No one comes to the Father except through me" (John 14:6). Even today, Jesus remains the one on whom we focus all our attention, and the place where we find him revealed to us is Scripture. Our fourth Article of Faith, "The Holy Scriptures," reminds us:

> We believe in the plenary inspiration of the Holy Scriptures, by which we understand the 66 books of the Old and New Testaments, given by divine inspiration, inerrantly revealing the will of God concerning us in all things necessary to our salvation, so that whatever is not contained therein is not to be enjoined as an article of faith.[18]

Albert Outler was a Wesleyan/Methodist theologian of the twentieth century who coined the phrase "the Wesleyan quadrilateral" as a way of defining what he saw as John Wesley's method for theologizing. John Wesley, in Outler's opinion, utilized Scripture, church tradition, reason, and experience[19] as his theological paradigm.[20] Dr. Tom Noble[21] reminds us that

---

18. Church of the Nazarene, "Article IV: The Holy Scriptures," *Manual: 2023*, 27.

19. Experience in the way Wesley and Outler understood it is not about personal individual experiences but communal experiences as mediated through the church, which includes the larger body of Christ.

20. Albert C. Outler, ed., *John Wesley* (Oxford: Oxford University Press, 1964), iv.

21. Thomas A. Noble has served as research professor of theology at Nazarene Theological Seminary in Kansas City, where he taught for

Introduction

"the so-called quadrilateral is not a quadrilateral, if that is taken to imply, as it appears to, four more or less equal factors, or four factors on the same level. Where it is really misleading is when the four factors are regarded as four distinct sources of doctrine."[22] Early Nazarene historian Dr. Timothy Smith suggested we consider a stool in place of a quadrilateral. Scripture then becomes the floor on which the stool stands as the foundation of doctrine. "Doctrine itself is the seat of the stool, standing on this scriptural foundation on three legs, tradition, experience, and reason. The three 'legs' then are figurative for the way we interpret Scripture."[23] We must recognize the importance of Scripture as the foundation upon which everything else stands.

Within those scriptures, we find the Ten Commandments in Exodus 20:3–4, 7, 8, 12–17):

You shall have no other gods before me.

You shall not make for yourself an image in the form of anything in heaven above or on the earth beneath or in the waters below.

You shall not misuse the name of the Lord your God, for the Lord will not hold anyone guiltless who misuses his name.

Remember the Sabbath day by keeping it holy.

---

twenty-five years. Before that, he taught theology at Nazarene Theological College in Manchester, where he is still a research fellow, supervising PhD research with the University of Manchester. He is a graduate of the Universities of Glasgow (MA) and Edinburgh (BD, PhD) and a past president of the Wesleyan Theological Society and of the T. F. Torrance Theological Fellowship.

22. T. A. Noble, *Holy Trinity, Holy People: The Theology of Christian Perfecting* (Eugene, OR: Cascade Books, 2013), Kindle Location 479.

23. Noble, *Holy Trinity, Holy People*, Kindle Location 479.

Honor your father and your mother, so that you may live long in the land the LORD your God is giving you.
You shall not murder.
You shall not commit adultery.
You shall not steal.
You shall not give false testimony against your neighbor.
You shall not covet your neighbor's house. You shall not covet your neighbor's wife, or his male or female servant, his ox or donkey, or anything that belongs to your neighbor."

These commandments were reaffirmed in and through the teachings of Jesus, who came not only to fulfill the old law but also to usher in a new covenant. In fulfilling the law, Jesus did not cast off Moses, but through his life and ministry he became the fulfillment of the prophetic words of Jeremiah. The law would now be written on the hearts of God's people, rather than on tablets of stone (see Jer. 31:31–34). All of this would be made possible through the indwelling of the Holy Spirit. This was the beautiful promise of Jesus—that the indwelling of the Spirit would be possible and that, even though Jesus might not be with them in the flesh, the Advocate would continue to teach and mold them in their life of discipleship.

John 14:26

But the Advocate, the Holy Spirit, whom the Father will send in my name, will teach you all things and will remind you of everything I have said to you.

John 16:13

But when he, the Spirit of truth, comes, he will guide you into all the truth. He will not speak on his own; he will speak only what he hears, and he will tell you what is yet to come.

Introduction

Although the disciples didn't understand what these words about the Holy Spirit meant at the time, things would come into focus for them on the day of Pentecost. In the meantime, they had Jesus to teach and mentor them. Throughout their time following Jesus, they were being shaped into reflections of him.

The disciples' understanding of the fulfillment of the law became abundantly clear when Jesus was questioned by an expert in the law. The result is what has come to be known as the Greatest Commandment. Matthew 22:35–40 tells us of the conversation:

> One of them, an expert in the law, tested him with this question: "Teacher, which is the greatest commandment in the Law?"
>
> Jesus replied: "'Love the Lord your God with all your heart and with all your soul and with all your mind.' This is the first and greatest commandment. And the second is like it: 'Love your neighbor as yourself.' All the Law and the Prophets hang on these two commandments."

This commandment is reiterated in the Gospels of Mark and Luke as well (see Mark 12:28–31; Luke 10:25–28). Jesus was summarizing the ethical teaching of the Ten Commandments by sorting them into two relational categories. One had to do with how we relate to God, and the other had to do with how we relate to people. The disciples were to be in a holy relationship with God through Christ Jesus and also with one another through the power and presence of the Holy Spirit. Jesus promised that the presence of the Holy Spirit would go with them and help them in the days ahead.

INTRODUCTION

The Sermon on the Mount was seminal in the formation of Jesus's disciples. Found in Matthew 5–7, this sermon emphasizes Jesus's moral teachings. In the fifth century, Augustine wrote:

> If anyone will piously and soberly consider the sermon which our Lord Jesus Christ spoke on the mount, as we read it in the Gospel according to Matthew, I think that he will find in it, so far as regards the highest morals, a perfect standard of the Christian life.[24]

The early church was grappling with standards for the Christian life, and they continually returned to the Sermon on the Mount. Thus, we too, return to Jesus's sermon, and there find a way forward for us as a people called Nazarene.

◆ **28.2. God invites us to join in his work of restoration through commitment to wholeness. Thus, our shared conviction is that the Christian life will mean continually 'putting on' some things and 'laying down' others. Such practices are often sacrificial, and shape us for a life of witness in the world in which we live. These move believers toward ever-increasing Christlikeness, are intentional, and develop over time as people discern and respond to God's call to participate in Christ.**
(Gen. 2:1–3; Exod. 20:8–11; Lev. 25:1–5; 1 Thess. 5:23)

The very first Article of Faith in the Nazarene *Manual* is about the triune God: "We believe in one eternally existent, infinite God, Sovereign Creator and Sustainer of the universe; that he only is God, holy in nature, attributes, and purpose.

---

24. Augustine, *Nicene and Post-Nicene Fathers: Series I/Volume VI/ Our Lord's Sermon on the Mount/Book I.*

Introduction

The God who is holy love and light is triune in essential being, revealed as Father, Son, and Holy Spirit."[25]

The holy love bound up in God the Father, Son, and Holy Spirit characterizes our life when we become partakers of the divine nature (see 2 Pet. 1:4). Love is to be the rule of our relationship with the triune God, and this is made possible through something that has become known as *perichoresis*. Originally the term meant "to go around" something, or "to rotate" something. However, when the term was used by a fourth-century theologian, it became a way to understand Christ and the relationship within the triune God. The term took on an understanding of "interpenetration and was an expression of how the divinity and humanity of Christ coinhered."[26] It is because of this interpenetration of the human and the divine in Christ that humans are invited to become part of the loving relationship found in the triune God.[27] When the image of God is restored in humanity, then "created being mirrors the Uncreated."[28] Because of this *perichoresis*, we can experience the indwelling of the triune God, which Jesus promised in John 14:23: "Anyone who loves me will obey my teaching. My Father will love them, and we will come to them and make our home with them." It is precisely in this manner that we are invited to participate in Christ, and he in us.

---

25. Church of the Nazarene, "Article I: The Triune God," *Manual: 2023*, 26.

26. F. W. Norris, "Deification," 416. He is referring to Nazianzen, Or. 18.42; Or 22.4; Ep.101.31; and finally Athanasius, *Discourse Against the Arians* 3.1, 17, 19, 24–25.

27. Carla D. Sunberg, *The Cappadocian Mothers: Deification Exemplified in the Writings of Basil, Gregory, and Gregory* (Eugene, OR: Pickwick Publications, 2018), 71.

28. Daniel F. Stramara, "Gregory of Nyssa's Terminology," 263.

INTRODUCTION

To participate in Christ is to take on the whole of what Christ has to offer us. As God's people, restoration comes from all that God provides us through a relationship of holy love. One of the ways the early members of the Church of the Nazarene found wholeness was through the embrace of sabbath. There is something significant about God's plan for humanity that includes a time for rest, and in that rest, we find restoration.

Genesis 2:1–3

Thus the heavens and the earth were completed in all their vast array. By the seventh day God had finished the work he had been doing; so on the seventh day he rested from all his work. Then God blessed the seventh day and made it holy, because on it he rested from all the work of creating that he had done.

Exodus 20:8–11

Remember the Sabbath day by keeping it holy. Six days you shall labor and do all your work, but the seventh day is a sabbath to the LORD your God. On it you shall not do any work, neither you, nor your son or daughter, nor your male or female servant, nor your animals, nor any foreigner residing in your towns. For in six days the LORD made the heavens and the earth, the sea, and all that is in them, but he rested on the seventh day. Therefore the LORD blessed the Sabbath day and made it holy.

Leviticus 25:1–5

The LORD said to Moses at Mount Sinai, "Speak to the Israelites and say to them: 'When you enter the land I am going to give you, the land itself must observe a sabbath to the LORD. For six years sow your fields, and for six years prune your vineyards and gather their crops. But in the seventh year the land is to have a year of sabbath rest, a sabbath to the LORD. *Do not sow your fields or prune your vineyards. Do not reap what grows of itself or harvest the grapes of your untended vines. The land is to have a year of rest.*

Interestingly, these passages on sabbath give us an understanding of putting some things on and taking off others. The putting on had to do with the labors in which they were to participate. In Genesis, God was active in the work of creation. The work that God took on was immense as the entire world was filled with every minute detail of this divine achievement. In Exodus, we read about the work that God's people would do for six days. Leviticus gives us a few more details of that work, which included sowing, pruning, and the gathering of crops. All of this encompassed a great deal of taking on responsibility and activity.

In contrast, God also commanded the people to rest. This could be interpreted as the taking off of some things, and if God needed to take some things off, maybe we do as well. This may underscore why the early Nazarenes felt that the practice of sabbath rest was vitally important to the faith. It may have had a great deal to do with the embrace of putting on and taking off and finding restoration, or wholeness, in Christ.

1 Thessalonians 5:23

May God himself, the God of peace, sanctify you through and through. May your whole spirit, soul and body be kept blameless at the coming of our Lord Jesus Christ.

INTRODUCTION

Our putting on and laying down and our embrace of sabbath are possible because the Holy Spirit is working, saturating our being by sanctifying us through and through.

As we work through the rest of this section of the covenant about The Christian Life, we will reflect on the things *to* which we are called and those things *from* which we are called. Just as God models this example through Sabbath keeping, we intentionally choose to sacrifice so that our lives may serve as witnesses for Christ.

Questions for Reflection

1. Consider how your life has changed since coming to Christ. What kinds of things have you put on, and what have you taken off?

2. How do you see the call to holiness informing the Christian life?

3. How might we be tempted to live under what Bonhoeffer called cheap grace? What are the consequences?

4. The Sermon on the Mount calls us to a new way of living. What challenges you from that message?

5. Why do you think the early Nazarenes were concerned about the keeping of the Sabbath? How are we doing with Sabbath keeping today? How might we need to rethink our own practices?

SECTION I
We Are Called To . . .

1
DISCIPLESHIP WITHIN THE FAMILY OF GOD (¶28.3)

◆ 28.3. We call our people to discipleship in the context of faithful congregations. Nurture, grace, and accountability are the responsibility of the Christian community. As the family of God, we take seriously the responsibility to raise children into Christlikeness, teaching them from birth that they are recipients of the fullness of Jesus' love. We are called to become the family of God for those who have never experienced the love of Jesus.
(1 Cor. 12:27–28; Eph. 2:14–16)

The Church of the Nazarene is an intentionally connectional community, united as one global family. From the earliest days of the Wesleyan movement, we have been a people who have practiced our faith within a community that helped shape and form our discipleship. John Wesley had small groups known as bands and classes, where people met regularly for accountability and spiritual growth. Sadly, we can find ourselves tempted to step away from the group and think we can grow on our own spiritually. The reality is that every local congregation should be engaged in the discipleship formation of their members.

SECTION I

Corporate worship is a joy and a regular practice of our congregations, and although it is vitally important to the life of the church, at the core of a Wesleyan-Holiness understanding, there must be space created for discipleship. If we are to take seriously our mission to make Christlike disciples in the nations, then our time and energy should be spent nurturing those who are growing in grace, which includes all of us. Discipleship occurs in small groups and in the development of a devotional life that includes prayer and the study of Scripture.

1 Corinthians 12:27-28

Now you are the body of Christ, and each one of you is a part of it. And God has placed in the church first of all apostles, second prophets, third teachers, then miracles, then gifts of healing, of helping, of guidance, and of different kinds of tongues.

Understanding the body of Christ and functioning within that body is important to the Christian life. The church in Corinth was going through a time of great difficulty, for there were those who were displaying spiritual gifts that were creating division in the church. The more flamboyant gifts were getting the attention of the people. Suddenly, God was performing miracles through some of the individuals, and the congregations saw a great many people healed.

Some were speaking in tongues; there continues to be much discussion to this day over what exactly Paul was talking about in the use of the word "tongues."[1] Most commentators say he meant diverse languages. In the cosmopolitan city of

---

1. As a denomination, Nazarenes do not affirm the spiritual gift of speaking in tongues because we believe God wants to be understood by everyone, without an intermediary beyond the Son and the Holy Spirit.

Corinth—a crossroads for much of the world—the ability to speak in multiple languages would indeed be a gift, and the ability to interpret multiple languages carried power. If you've ever spoken through a translator, you understand that you are at the mercy of your interpreter, and you trust that your words will be conveyed in the manner you have intended. What we do know is that those who had the more outwardly exciting gifts were using them as proof that they were more spiritual than others in the church. The result was a divided church.

Paul decided to bring some order to the chaos the church in Corinth was experiencing. Several times in 1 Corinthians 12, he refers to different people with varying gifts. Finally, at the end, he points out a hierarchy for authority and/or structure within the church. He ends with three groupings, wanting to make clear that outward acts do not necessarily equal greater authority.

The first category of leadership came from apostles, prophets, and teachers. The apostles included the original twelve followers of Jesus, but also the sent seventy, and this grouping eventually also included people like Paul, Barnabas, Andronicus, and Junia. In the first century, apostles were those who had actually seen Christ and were carrying the news about him to the world. Also included in this first leadership category were the prophets, or the preachers—those who had not seen Christ but were preachers and champions of the gospel. This would include individuals like Apollos, the daughters of Philip, and others who traveled the known world preaching about Christ. But even Apollos had some issues with his theology and had to come under the authority of other teachers like Priscilla and Aquila, who help Apollos understand that sometimes his preaching wasn't quite right. These groups would all be found in the first category. Paul was saying that, while you may not be seeing charismatic gifts from these leaders, God has placed them in authority, and this is their gifting. Just because they don't have the other gifts does not mean they are not spiritual leaders.

Of course, with leadership authority came great responsibility. These early church leaders were actively engaged in the crucial task of discipling the next generation of leaders. If the baton were dropped, it could spell the end of Christianity; therefore, they went out and followed Jesus's command to make disciples. Paul had Barnabas; John had Ignatius and Polycarp; and Peter had Mark. Everywhere we read in the New Testament, the community of believers was becoming a new family for those who were coming to Christ, and actively discipling the next generation.

Next in Paul's list came those who performed miracles and exercised gifts of healing. It seems apparent that God was giving this gift to a number of individuals. It was exciting to see God pouring out his Spirit and working in this way, and crowds gathered to watch those who had these spiritual gifts. However, with the crowds came temptation. When people start showering you with praise, you might begin to think you are more popular, more important, and more gifted for leadership than those in authority. The real danger comes when those with such gifts try to seize leadership. Paul served as the spiritual father to these individuals and left them with a reminder that visible spiritual gifts are not necessarily a sign of higher spiritual maturity. This is why the Christian life has to be practiced in community, where there is accountability and teaching from those who are more mature in the faith.

The final group of people in the church included those with gifts for helping, administration, and various tongues. This would include those with practical skills to help out in the church: the worker bees, administrators, church treasurers, translators, and more. They loved to keep all the pieces together and going, and there surely were times when the prophetic types or the miracle types drove them up the wall! Why? Because the movement of the Holy Spirit can result in messy things, and they wanted to organize and plan it out a little better.

Paul was telling them that all of these gifts matter to God. They are all important in the church, but God wants the community to function in an orderly manner. They are to be a body, a community of faith whose main goal is to make disciples. Therefore, the church is to be well ordered so it can serve as a healthy community, nurturing new believers in the faith. This is the responsibility of the church, and it should not be taken for granted.

Ephesians 2:14–16

For he himself is our peace, who has made the two groups one and has destroyed the barrier, the dividing wall of hostility, by setting aside in his flesh the law with its commands and regulations. His purpose was to create in himself one new humanity out of the two, thus making peace, and in one body to reconcile both of them to God through the cross, by which he put to death their hostility.

The word "peace" has significance in understanding the place of community in the life of the believer. Interestingly, we understand that Christ has come not only to bring peace but also to bring us together as one. In the case of this Ephesians scripture, he has brought together the Jews and the gentiles, making them into one people. The family of God is not a place of division but a place where people from all walks of life can come together and find belonging. The coming together of different people groups creates new humanity, and the result is peace. This is why we need to live out our Christian life in community. At times it will be challenging, but it will also be what makes us the true people of God.

Raising children is the responsibility of parents, but it is also the responsibility of the church community. The Church of the Nazarene used to have a ministry called the Cradle Roll. Actually, since the late nineteenth century, this was an active ministry of nearly all Protestant denominations. These days, you will find it mentioned twice in the *Manual*, listed as a possible activity of the Children's Ministries Council of NDI, but with no explanation of its function. Originally, the ministry was designed for the church to be responsible for all children under the age of four who had any kind of connection to the local church. It may have included a church member's grandchild, or a child whose older siblings attended Vacation Bible School, or a sports program, or a child whose family did or did not attend regularly. It didn't matter because the local church took upon itself the responsibility to be engaged in the spiritual nurturing of that child. Sometimes the names of all the Cradle Roll children would be written on a baby shoe and posted on a bulletin board. Family members used to be given certificates so they knew their child was part of a local church's responsibility. Members of the congregation would take it upon themselves to check on those children on a regular basis and find ways to encourage the parents and offer to help bring those children to church. When the child turned four, they became an official part of the children's department at the church.

Historically, the church had lists of Sunday school enrollment that a teacher would receive. The teacher was encouraged to follow up regularly with those assigned to their class. Over the years, some felt that these lists needed to be cleaned up to reflect only those who came on a regular basis. Shortly after the Second World War, Dr. Albert Harper became the director of Church Schools for the Church of the Nazarene. He helped redefine what came to be known as the Responsibility List, today called the Accountability Care List. Instead of viewing the enrollment as an attendance sheet, Dr. Harper encouraged the church to see it as their discipleship *responsibility*. The list was to be filled with as many names as that local church might include in their reach. Dr. Harper encouraged church workers to reach out to these individuals at least a couple times a month, whether they attended church or not. His rule of thumb was that a local church would probably have about half as many people in attendance as they had on their responsibility list. His concern with cleaning up the rolls was that the church was actually reducing their reach and their responsibility for those whom God had placed within their sphere of influence. Today, we embrace this list as the Accountability Care List, recognizing that we should take responsibility for the lives of all whom God has given us the ability to influence for him.

Within the church's sphere of influence, we find both single and married parents. Parenting is a difficult task, especially when there is not a good support system or when there hasn't been good modeling by the previous generation. The church has a responsibility to come alongside parents to help equip them to raise their children as followers of Jesus Christ.

Throughout history, the home has been a powerful place of discipleship. In the early eighteenth century, Susanna Wesley became one of the most influential leaders in Christianity—not by her direct preaching or teaching but by the way she raised her children. Having given birth to twenty children, ten of whom reached adulthood, this wife of a poor preacher invested in the lives of her children, wanting them to know as much about Christ as possible. She believed it was her responsibility to ground them in the faith, and she did. Every child was given one hour a week of one-on-one time with their mother, during which she carefully adapted her teaching to each of their needs. The children learned scriptures, songs and hymns, and how to pray. All of this happened at home, and two of Susanna's sons, John and Charles, went on to become the founders of the Methodist movement that today has more than eighty million adherents and has had a profound impact on our world. Susanna was trained in the faith by her own parents and by the church in which she was raised. This partnership between church and parent made the difference in the discipleship of her children.

In his first letter to the church in Corinth, Paul notes that singleness is a gift from God: "I wish that all of you were as I am. But each of you has your own gift from God; one has this gift, another has that" (1 Cor. 7:7). The church has often emphasized the place of marriage and family in the community of discipleship but has failed to note the gift that singleness is to the church. Throughout history, some of our greatest leaders have been single. Whether the apostle Paul, or Macrina and her brother, Basil, of the fourth century, they all adopted a way of life in which they practiced celibacy and chose to remain single. In the Church of the Nazarene, we have had significant missionary leaders who chose service to Christ over marrying and having a family. But these members of our community also need family, which is the responsibility of the church. The church family ought to be a home where the love of Jesus is experienced in practical ways, caring for one another in times of need and in times of joy. Being a family encompasses more than just funerals and Christmas dinners; it requires an invitation into the daily rhythm of life.

Focusing on the discipleship of the church family across the generations is vitally important. At the same time, as we take into account the journey of grace, it is our hope and prayer that the community of faith becomes a family that exhibits grace to those who may not know the love of Jesus. We are called to be channels of prevenient grace for those who have not yet experienced the saving and sanctifying grace of our Lord. Congregations may need to wrestle with what it looks like to welcome the stranger into their family, where Jesus's love can be experienced.

May our churches and homes always be ready to celebrate those whom God sends our way. With tables spread and warm embraces, may we reflect the love of the triune God in and through our communities of faith.

SECTION I

Questions for Reflection

1. Why is it important to practice our discipleship within a community of faith?

2. How has your church provided for communities of accountability and discipleship formation?

3. What is the danger of having outward and more "exciting" spiritual gifts?

2
ENGAGE IN RECONCILING LOVE (¶28.4)

◆ 28.4. We call our people to proclaim and demonstrate God's grace and love to the world. Equipping believers for reconciling love as ambassadors for Christ in the world is the shared responsibility of every congregation. God calls us to attitudes, practices of hospitality, and relationships that value all persons. We participate as joyful disciples, engaging with others to create a society that mirrors God's purposes. Our faith is to work through love. Therefore, the church is to give herself to the care, feeding, clothing, and shelter of the poor and marginalized. A life of Christian holiness will entail efforts to create a more just and equitable society and world, especially for the poor, the oppressed, and those who cannot speak for themselves.

(Lev. 19:18, 34; Deut. 15:7–8, 11; Isa. 61:1; Zech. 9:12; Matt. 25:34–46; Rom. 5:7–8; 12:1; 2 Cor. 5:16, 20; Gal. 5:6; Eph. 2:10; 6:12; Phil. 2:5–11; Col. 1:27; James 2:1–9)

The work of Christ was that of reconciling love. Therefore, if we are called to follow him and be his disciples, then we are called to participate in this same work. The sheer number of passages supporting this call to engage in reconciling love bears witness to the overwhelming number of ways in which this is reflected in the character of the triune God and in the life of Christ.

Leviticus 19:18, 34

Do not seek revenge or bear a grudge against anyone among your people, but love your neighbor as yourself. I am the LORD.

The foreigner residing among you must be treated as your native-born. Love them as yourself, for you were foreigners in Egypt. I am the LORD your God.

The children of Israel—God's chosen people—had foreigners living among them. God's plan was for his chosen people to be agents of reconciliation and evangelism. Through the Israelites, the world was to see what God's activity looked like. The word that permeates God's call to discipleship is *love*, and this is God's work.

Our world encourages us to seek revenge, or tells us we should seek justice for the wrongs we have experienced, but in one of the earliest books of the Bible, we are called to love our neighbors—especially when our neighbors are foreigners—as ourselves. We rarely get to choose our neighbors. They come with the communities we live in. We don't always know where they have come from, what traditions they bring with them, or how they may behave toward us, yet these details should not matter because everyone who becomes our neighbor is a gift to us from God.

The Salvation Army is known for its hospitality toward all people, and somehow they have found a way to manage their ministry without becoming embroiled in politics. When speaking about the massive movement of people around the world and ministering to migrants, Salvation Army leadership commented that they don't judge how people arrived where they are but simply look upon them as individuals who have a need, and they try to meet that need. Every person on this earth is valued as a child of God, and we are to love and respect those whom God puts in our path, no matter their place of origin.

Deuteronomy 15:7–8, 11

If anyone is poor among your fellow Israelites in any of the towns of the land the LORD *your God is giving you, do not be hardhearted or tightfisted toward them. Rather, be openhanded and freely lend them whatever they need.*

There will always be poor people in the land. Therefore I command you to be openhanded toward your fellow Israelites who are poor and needy in your land.

God's desire is that generosity toward the poor mark the people of God. There have been seasons when we have done better with this than others. In the fourth century, Christianity was gaining approval by the Roman government but was so effective at providing for the needs of widows, orphans, and the sick that they embarrassed Emperor Julian. He tried to encourage his governors to do more than the Christians, but they could not, and on his deathbed he reportedly declared, "You have won, Galilean!" or, as some have translated the Greek, "The Nazarene has won!"[1] The only way the Nazarene could have won was by overwhelming acts of generosity that superseded what could be provided by the empire. This is the moment in history that led to the tax-free status of the church.

---

1. First recorded by Theodoret in the fifth century. Theodoret, Hist. eccl. 3.25 (*NPNF* 7:196).

They were given this special freedom because they provided so many of the services the government was unable or unwilling to provide.

Isaiah 61:1

The Spirit of the Sovereign LORD *is on me,*
because the LORD *has anointed me*
to proclaim good news to the poor.
He has sent me to bind up the brokenhearted,
to proclaim freedom for the captives
and release from darkness for the prisoners.

Dr. Phineas F. Bresee, the founding father of the Church of the Nazarene in Los Angeles, was a Methodist minister and carried within him John Wesley's passion to spread scriptural holiness across the land. To this commitment he added a passion for ministering to the poor. The first Nazarene church in Los Angeles was organized on the third Sunday of October 1895. "At the morning service eighty-six men and women stood together and plighted to God and each other their fidelity in the organization and carrying on of the work of the Church of the Nazarene, with the declared purpose of preaching holiness, and carrying the gospel to the poor."[2] Within the DNA of the Church of the Nazarene we find instilled a specific call to minister to those on the margins of society. Because of this engagement in reconciling love, the 2023 edition of the *Manual* emphasizes ministry to the poor in the Covenant of Christian

---

2. E.A. Girvin, *Phineas F. Bresee, A Prince in Israel: A Biography* (Kansas City, MO: Nazarene Publishing House, 1981), 53.

Conduct. However, the following statement has already been in the appendix of the *Manual* since 2013:

> **917. Responsibility to the Poor.** The Church of the Nazarene believes that Jesus commanded his disciples to have a special relationship to the poor of this world; that Christ's church ought, first, to keep itself simple and free from an emphasis on wealth and extravagance and, second, to give itself to the care, feeding, clothing, and shelter of the poor. Throughout the Bible and in the life and example of Jesus, God identifies with and assists the poor, the oppressed, and those in society who cannot speak for themselves. In the same way, we too are called to identify with and to enter into solidarity with the poor and not simply to offer charity from positions of comfort. We hold that compassionate ministry to the poor includes acts of charity as well as a struggle to provide opportunity, equality, and justice for the poor. We further believe that the Christian responsibility to the poor is an essential aspect of the life of every believer who seeks a faith that works through love.
>
> Finally, we understand Christian holiness to be inseparable from ministry to the poor in that holiness compels the Christian beyond his or her own individual perfection and toward the creation of a more just and equitable society and world. Holiness, far from distancing believers from the desperate economic needs of people in our world, motivates us to place our means in the service of alleviating such need and to adjust our wants in accordance with the needs of others.
>
> (Exod. 23:11; Deut. 15:7; Ps. 41:1; 82:3; Prov. 19:17; 21:13; 22:9; Jer. 22:16; Matt. 19:21; Luke 12:33; Acts 20:35; 2 Cor. 9:6; Gal. 2:10)

As we can see, holiness and ministry to the poor are inseparable and are at the very heart of what it means to be a Nazarene because of our understanding of restoration, made possible by the power of the Holy Spirit. There is no reason that anyone must remain in their current condition because we are prisoners of hope.

Zechariah 9:12

Return to your fortress, you prisoners of hope;
even now I announce that I will restore twice as much to you.

Zechariah's prophetic words pointed to a time in the future when God's people would return to their homeland and again be free. They were prisoners of hope, for they knew that restoration was possible. Today, we do not have to wait for a future time of restoration, for that restoration has been made possible in the coming of Jesus's kingdom. Together with our Lord we pray, "Your kingdom come, your will be done on earth as it is in heaven" (Matt. 6:10). The breaking in of the kingdom of God discloses to us the restorative work of our Lord.

In contrast, we are increasingly told that we are to suffer the fate of our place or condition in this world. This state of being has never been the way of the Nazarene. We may have been born with challenges or disabilities or an inclination to addiction, but the promise from God is that we can be prisoners of hope and restored in the image of God. Even in this lifetime, we can be set free from "the sin that so easily entangles" (Heb. 12:1). God's people, living out the Christian life, are to be agents of restoration to those in need of a helping hand.

God takes this work of restoration so seriously that failing to participate in this activity has consequences, something about which Jesus was clear. Our next scripture indicates that there will come a day when the King examines and judges those he has left as stewards of his kingdom.

Matthew 25:34–46

Then the King will say to those on his right, "Come, you who are blessed by my Father; take your inheritance, the kingdom prepared for you since the creation of the world. For I was hungry and you gave me something to eat, I was thirsty and you gave me something to drink, I was a stranger and you invited me in, I needed clothes and you clothed me, I was sick and you looked after me, I was in prison and you came to visit me."

Then the righteous will answer him, "Lord, when did we see you hungry and feed you, or thirsty and give you something to drink? When did we see you a stranger and invite you in, or needing clothes and clothe you? When did we see you sick or in prison and go to visit you?"

The King will reply, "Truly I tell you, whatever you did for one of the least of these brothers and sisters of mine, you did for me."

Then he will say to those on his left, "Depart from me, you who are cursed, into the eternal fire prepared for the devil and his angels. For I was hungry and you gave me nothing to eat, I was thirsty and you gave me nothing to drink, I was a stranger and you did not invite me in, I needed clothes and you did not clothe me, I was sick and in prison and you did not look after me."

They also will answer, "Lord, when did we see you hungry or thirsty or a stranger or needing clothes or sick or in prison, and did not help you?"

He will reply, "Truly I tell you, whatever you did not do for one of the least of these, you did not do for me."

SECTION I

Then they will go away to eternal punishment, but the righteous to eternal life.

This passage was a very sober teaching from Jesus. He expected his disciples to be transformed and live in a way that reflected him. On our spiritual journey, we will encounter people who may be a challenge to love. The question is, "Where do you see Jesus?" We may convince ourselves that we can't impact the life of the beggar on the street, but maybe it's not all about them but about what we would do for Christ.

Dr. Chic Shaver taught evangelism at Nazarene Theological Seminary, and he prodded his students to have "evangelism eyes"—to ask Jesus to help them see the world the way Jesus does. Through prayer, our eyes are opened, and we are no longer blinded by the need, but, clear-eyed, we see the person. Then we can minister in the name of Jesus.

Romans 5:7-8; 12:1

Very rarely will anyone die for a righteous person, though for a good person someone might possibly dare to die. But God demonstrates his own love for us in this: While we were still sinners, Christ died for us.

Therefore, I urge you, brothers and sisters, in view of God's mercy, to offer your bodies as a living sacrifice, holy and pleasing to God—this is your true and proper worship.

Ministering in the name of Jesus is not always easy, and not everyone is likeable or righteous. Jesus gave himself as a living sacrifice, and the call to follow him is costly. We, too, are to sacrifice for the sake of others, even those who may not be deserving in our eyes. We weren't deserving of God's grace when Christ died for us. Therefore, we can't expect others to be deserving of grace either. Jesus tells us, "Give, and it will be given to you. . . . For with the measure you use, it will be measured to you" (Luke 6:38).

So, since we are now followers of Jesus Christ, Paul reminds us with the next scripture that we will have a different point of view, or perspective, on things.

2 Corinthians 5:16, 20

So from now on we regard no one from a worldly point of view. Though we once regarded Christ in this way, we do so no longer.

We are therefore Christ's ambassadors, as though God were making his appeal through us. We implore you on Christ's behalf: Be reconciled to God.

As we live out the Christian life, we take on the new role and responsibility of ambassador. Almost every country has ambassadors who are sent to other nations to represent the home country. The embassy, while located in a foreign land, is considered territory of the nation it represents. The ambassador does not speak for him or herself but represents the leadership of their nation in all things, including official functions but also the mundane. It may be a formal state dinner or an informal birthday party for children, but the ambassador is always on duty, representing their nation.

As Christians, we become ambassadors for Christ, representing him in the embassy of his kingdom on earth. We are on duty as his agents of reconciliation, whether at official church functions or informal neighborhood parties. Our faith is to be reflected in all that we do, and always through love.

SECTION I

Galatians 5:6

For in Christ Jesus neither circumcision nor uncircumcision has any value. The only thing that counts is faith expressing itself through love.

It was far too easy for the early Christians to judge others, specifically in regard to their spiritual lives. The Jews looked down on the gentiles. Jews had always tried to live moral lives, and what they perceived as the immorality of the gentiles was hard for them to bear.

In a similar way, those who have been in the church for a long time may struggle with new believers, who still have much to learn. Disciples who have been following Jesus for a long time don't score more points than those who have just started. Paul says the only thing that counts is faith expressing itself through love. Those who have gone to church for a long time may struggle with expressing love. Sometimes we are unaware that we have become side-tracked on our journey and that, instead of continuing to grow in grace, our hearts have hardened. The good news is that grace is continually extended to us, and we can get back up, knock the dust from our knees, and get going again. Jesus is always there, hand extended, waiting to lead us. His love compels us to keep moving, and once we do, our faith will again be expressed in love, for this is how we have been created.

Ephesians 2:10; 6:12

For we are God's handiwork, created in Christ Jesus to do good works, which God prepared in advance for us to do.

For our struggle is not against flesh and blood, but against the rulers, against the authorities, against the powers of this dark world and against the spiritual forces of evil in the heavenly realms.

God, in the beauty of creation, had a plan for us to reflect his image to the world. If Jesus participated in good works, then we are to participate in good works. We do not do it in order to earn our salvation, but it is the work of a disciple. Through the incarnation—Christ coming in human flesh—the doorway was opened to our participation in the triune God.

We have mentioned previously the opportunity to become partakers of the divine nature. In this scripture and the next, Paul tells us we are to have the same mindset as that of Christ, which is only possible because of what Christ has done for us, and through the presence of the Holy Spirit. We follow Jesus into holy intimacy with God, and we are changed. That's why Paul wrote the ancient hymn to the church in Philippi.

Philippians 2:5-11

In your relationships with one another, have the same mindset as Christ Jesus: Who, being in very nature God, did not consider equality with God something to be used to his own advantage; rather, he made himself nothing by taking the very nature of a servant, being made in human likeness. And being found in appearance as a man, he humbled himself by becoming obedient to death—even death on a cross! Therefore God exalted him to the highest place and gave him the name that is above every name, that at the name of Jesus every knee should bow, in heaven and on earth and under the earth, and every tongue acknowledge that Jesus Christ is Lord, to the glory of God the Father.

This passage that we often call the Christ Hymn ends with a crescendo of praise that gives glory to the Father. Our lives—the Christian life—glorify the Father because of how we live. We who are prisoners of hope have Christ in us, and this is the hope of glory.

Colossians 1:27

To them God has chosen to make known among the Gentiles the glorious riches of this mystery, which is Christ in you, the hope of glory.

We must consider whom we are welcoming into our churches. Dr. Bresee was "convinced that houses of worship should be plain and cheap, to save from financial burdens, and that everything should say welcome to the poor."[3] The church provided food, clothing, and shelter for the needy of the city. The front rows at Los Angeles First Church of the Nazarene were saved for the poorest of the poor, "the only condition being that they come early enough to get there."[4]

Often, when you visit an older town or city in the United States, you will find a downtown dotted with churches, sometimes four different ones at an intersection. Interestingly, you usually won't find the Church of the Nazarene there because our call was not to the busy downtown but to the people on the margins, often in the poorer parts of town. As the church grew and developed, even Bresee saw the needs of every community and recognized that ministry would reach beyond the poor, but

---

3. Girvin, *Phineas F. Bresee*, 77.
4. Girvin, *Phineas F. Bresee*, 77.

he always called the Nazarenes back to those with the greatest need.

Nazarene Compassionate Ministries (NCM) has become a channel through which Nazarenes collectively are able to minister to those who find themselves in crisis. At the same time, NCM works to urge every local church to reflect the love of Jesus within their own community.

James 2:1–9

My brothers and sisters, believers in our glorious Lord Jesus Christ must not show favoritism. Suppose a man comes into your meeting wearing a gold ring and fine clothes, and a poor man in filthy old clothes also comes in. If you show special attention to the man wearing fine clothes and say, "Here's a good seat for you," but say to the poor man, "You stand there" or "Sit on the floor by my feet," have you not discriminated among yourselves and become judges with evil thoughts?

Listen, my dear brothers and sisters: Has not God chosen those who are poor in the eyes of the world to be rich in faith and to inherit the kingdom he promised those who love him? But you have dishonored the poor. Is it not the rich who are exploiting you? Are they not the ones who are dragging you into court? Are they not the ones who are blaspheming the noble name of him to whom you belong?

If you really keep the royal law found in Scripture, "Love your neighbor as yourself," you are doing right. But if you show favoritism, you sin and are convicted by the law as lawbreakers.

To be engaged in reconciling love brings us full circle, for when we look to the left and to the right, we see our neighbor. One neighbor may be easier to love than the other, but we are not to show favoritism. Sometimes it is a lot easier to give to charitable organizations than it is to love the neighbors God has brought to our own communities. As the family of God, we are called to love our neighbors—even those whom we have not chosen. Not only are we to love them, but we are also to speak up for them and seek biblical justice for them so they may live in a world where we will all be treated as sisters and brothers in Christ.

Questions for Reflection

1. What does it look like for your church to be a channel of prevenient grace for those who need to know the transformational work of the Holy Spirit?

2. How are you ministering to those you see with the eyes of Christ?

3. What changes toward reconciling love do you or your church need to consider making?

3
CONSECRATE OUR TIME TO GOD (¶28.5)

◆ 28.5. We call our people to remember that all time is God's. The entirety of our lives should serve God's purposes. The way we use time impacts others, so together we commit to using time in ways that proclaim God's love to the world, build each other up, and craft healthy communities of grace. In this way, our leisure time, our active time, our sleep time, our work time, our worship time, and our whole time is offered in stewardship to God.
(Eph. 5:14–16)

Some of our African brothers and sisters have been known to tell their Christian siblings from the northern hemisphere, "You may have the watches, but we have the time." There are different understandings of time, even in the Bible, where we find two distinct words for time. One word is *chronos*, which is where we get the idea of chronology—what we measure by our watches. The other word is *kairos*, which is time as God measures it. Both *chronos* time and *kairos* time belong to God. Therefore, we give our time and our opportunity back to God as our worship and our stewardship of the time he has gifted to us.

SECTION I

Ephesians 5:14-16

This is why it is said: "Wake up, sleeper, rise from the dead, and Christ will shine on you." Be very careful, then, how you live—not as unwise but as wise, making the most of every opportunity, because the days are evil.

Since the turn of the twenty-first century, the advent of handheld electronic devices has had a major impact on our use of time. Worldwide, users of electronic devices aged sixteen to sixty-four are spending six hours and forty minutes a day on screens.[1] A study in the UK reported, "Screen time is prospectively associated with a range of mental health symptoms, especially depressive symptoms, though effect sizes are small. Video chat, texting, videos, and video games were the screen types with the greatest associations with depressive symptoms."[2] This admonition from the apostle Paul to make the most of every opportunity is useful for our day and age. As we journey on this Christian life, we must consider how we are using our time, and the greatest abuse of our time may be found in our own hands.

Dr. Bresee was conscientious about how he used his time; he felt it reflected the character of Christ. We have this glimpse

---

1. Simon Kemp, "Digital 2024: Global Overview Report," DataReportal, January 31, 2024, https://datareportal.com/reports/digital-2024-global-overview-report.

2. Jason M. Nagata, Abubakr A. A. Al-Shoaibi, Alicia W. Leong, Gabriel Zamora, Alexander Testa, Kyle T. Ganson, and Fiona C. Baker, "Screen time and mental health: a prospective analysis of the Adolescent Brain Cognitive Development (ABCD) Study," *BMC Public Health* 24, 2686 (2024), https://bmcpublichealth.biomedcentral.com/articles/10.1186/s12889-024-20102-x.

into the ways Bresee considered time from his biographer, Rev. Girvin:

> Dr. Bresee was hardly ever in a hurry, or greatly pressed for time. He carefully planned to meet all his appointments on time. He possessed singular precision. He saw a long way ahead, and allowed himself ample time for preparation. It could be truthfully said of him that he was never late at a religious service, and never missed a boat or other public conveyance. He allowed himself a sufficient margin, and enjoyed his spare time, not before he started, but after he had boarded his train. I have been in his home when the time came to start for church. He would say: "Everybody who is going to church get ready." Then he would put on his own hat and overcoat, and stand in an attitude of brisk expectancy until the others were ready. If they showed any signs of lagging, he had a pleasant but effective way of stirring them into action.[3]

He understood that the way he used his time would have an impact on others. As a leader in the church, he knew he always had to be ready for ministry, so he planned his preparation time. He also understood that not being on time for transportation would put out others. If he arrived late for a service or a gathering, that would certainly make things difficult for those who had worked to care for the details of the meeting. At the same time, we have the sense that he was able to relax and enjoy himself when the time allowed. Quite possibly, he could enjoy those times because he managed the remainder of his time well.

---

3. Girvin, *Phineas F. Bresee*, 162.

We live and worship in communities of grace, and we work to make these communities healthy. Wesley's band and class meetings were places of accountability, where the community both confessed to one another and encouraged one another to find wholeness, including in the use of time, which was to be stewarded well. In Proverbs we read of the one who does not use time wisely. The label "sluggard" is sometimes translated "lazy man."

- *A sluggard's appetite is never filled, but the desires of the diligent are fully satisfied (Prov. 13:4).*
- *Sluggards do not plow in season; so at harvest time they look but find nothing (Prov. 20:4).*
- *Those who work their land will have abundant food, but those who chase fantasies will have their fill of poverty (Prov. 28:19).*

The temptation to waste time, or use it unwisely, has always existed, and accountability among others in the community may be very useful.

Of course, cultural perspectives on time vary. Again, the northern hemisphere brings one understanding of time while the southern hemisphere glories in the *kairos* of God. In Ecclesiastes 3:11 we read about God's *kairos* time: "He has made everything beautiful in its time. He has also set eternity in the human heart; yet no one can fathom what God has done from beginning to end." There is something transcendent about God's time that we cannot fully comprehend. When we try to put God's *kairos* time into our *chronos* time, we may become frustrated. That is why learning from those who have come to relax in God's time is healthy. Our lives do not have to be ruled by the "tyranny of the urgent," a phrase coined by Charles Hummel, who comments on Jesus's use of time:

What was the secret of Jesus' work? We find a clue following Mark's account of Jesus' busy day. Mark observes that "in the morning, a great while before day, He rose and went out to a lonely place, and there He prayed" (Mark 1:35, RSV). Here is the secret of Jesus' life and work for God: He prayerfully waited for his Father's instructions and for the strength to follow them. Jesus had no divinely drawn blueprint; he discerned the Father's will day by day in a life of prayer. By this means he warded off the urgent and accomplished the important.[4]

Japanese theologian Kosuke Koyama reminds us that God is not necessarily in a hurry:

God walks "slowly" because he is love. If he is not love he would have gone much faster. Love has its speed. It is an inner speed. It is a spiritual speed. It is a different kind of speed from the technological speed to which we are accustomed. It is "slow" yet it is lord over all other speeds since it is the speed of love. It goes on in the depth of our life, whether we notice or not, whether we are currently hit by storm or not, at three miles an hour. It is the speed we walk and therefore it is the speed the love of God walks.[5]

We learn to give God our *chronos* and our *kairos*, and in doing so, the way we live our lives, and our time, are given over to God every day.

---

4. Charles Hummel, *Tyranny of the Urgent* (Downers Grove, IL: IVP, 1967), https://www.cslewisinstitute.org/wp-content/uploads/Tyranny-of-the-Urgent-Hummel-Fellows-Reading.pdf.

5. Kosuke Koyama, *Three Mile an Hour God* (London: SCM Press, 1979), 16–17.

SECTION I

Questions for Reflection

1. What does it mean to consecrate your time to God? What would that look like in your own life?

2. Reflect on your personal use of time. What changes do you need to make so you can more fully consecrate your time to God?

4
VALUE LEARNING (¶28.6)

◆ 28.6. We call our people to remember the value of learning. Education is of the utmost importance for the social and spiritual well-being of society. We call educational organizations and institutions to teach children, youth, and adults biblical principles and ethical standards in such a way that our doctrines may be known. Education from public sources should be complemented by Christian teaching in the home. Because all truth is God's truth, Christians should also be encouraged to work in and with public institutions to witness to and influence these institutions for God's kingdom.
(Matt. 5:13–14; Col. 1:16)

Before the Church of the Nazarene became a denomination, local churches and communities developed educational institutions, high schools, and Bible colleges. The concept of discipleship fueled the desire to have education available across the full age spectrum, from Sunday schools to the eventual creation of graduate institutions. Early Nazarene and other Holiness leaders believed education was a way to build the inner strength necessary to resist pressures from the world. The result was a strong commitment to the preaching and teaching of holiness at the core of all education.¹ The seriousness of educating our own young people was heavy on Dr. Bresee's heart:

> Especially is it necessary for us to educate our own youth. Spiritual religion is quite usually dispensed with, and often worse, in the colleges and universities of the land, and almost entirely holiness is tabooed and a seeker after it, or a professor of it, is regarded as a crank. At the age when the truth should be fixed in the mind and the experience developed toward maturity, their convictions are undermined, and their experience blasted. Academies and colleges are to us a necessity. Our young people will go forth to our pulpits, our counting houses, our farms, and our homes, full of the hallowed fire of the indwelling Spirit, only as they have been dwelling under the shadow of the Almighty in the classroom, chapel, and social life of their college years.²

The foundation for education was located in the message of holiness that permeated all understanding of discipleship and the Christian life. Both formal and nonformal education plays a key role in our being transformed into the likeness of Christ. This is because the renewing grace of God, through the power of the Holy Spirit, is at work in and through the educational process.

Education can enhance the life of a disciple to become the salt of the earth and the light of the world. This is one reason the Church of the Nazarene expanded beyond Bible colleges and developed liberal arts institutions. Because of the church's

---

1. Timothy L. Smith, *Called unto Holiness, Volume 1: The Story of the Nazarenes, the Formative Years* (Kansas City, MO: Beacon Hill Press, 1962), 273.

2. Girvin, *Phineas F. Bresee*, 215-16).

ministry to the poor, there has always been a desire to elevate people through education and to build into them the "habits, attitudes, and ideals" of those who have gone before them.[3]

Matthew 5:13-14

You are the salt of the earth. But if the salt loses its saltiness, how can it be made salty again? It is no longer good for anything, except to be thrown out and trampled underfoot. You are the light of the world. A town built on a hill cannot be hidden.

A number of years ago there was an incident on a lake in Louisiana. A petroleum company was drilling for oil beneath the lake. Unfortunately, they miscalculated the location for the shaft and drilled right into a salt dome, which opened up a hole into a salt mine. The lake began to drain into the salt mine below, making the salt hyper-saturated as it dissolved into the water and rendering both the water and the salt unusable. The situation then became much worse. Within a few hours the entire lake drained into the salt mine, along with some barges and an island. Finally, a geyser began to blow out of the salt mine shaft, and the area became a major ecological disaster that could not be repaired or corrected. Once the salt was ruined, it was ruined, and the domino effect was devastating.[4]

We are salt. As followers of Jesus Christ, we are to be pristine salt that provides a savory difference in the lives of those around us. We are to be genuine salt that, when sprinkled,

---

3. Smith, *Called unto Holiness, Volume 1*, 166.
4. John Pope, "An 'End of the World' Scene: Earth Swallows Lake, Oil Rig," *The Washington Post*, November 21, 1980, https://www.washingtonpost.com/archive/politics/1980/11/22/an-end-of-the-world-scene-earth-swallows-lake-oil-rig/2ad5eddb-fbe0-46d3-b8b3-db18bd3266ac/.

makes the world a better place. This is why education—helping us become the best we can be—is vitally important. This is not just about ministers; it is about all of us becoming the best humans reflecting the image of God that we can possibly be. Jesus was talking to those who were his followers and provided this gentle but understandable warning. It is possible to go from being good salt to bad salt, and it can happen when one rushes and is not careful. Again, this is the importance of taking time for an education.

Caring for our salty state or condition is discipleship. The picture is pretty clear for us; when our salt is ruined, we are no longer useful in the kingdom. If it is our desire to be good salt, then we must ask God by his grace to keep us in that place of saltiness. We keep learning, or else we may be like the men on the oil rig, drilling in the wrong place and creating a mess. The world needs to be seasoned by the saltiness of Jesus's disciples—therefore, we commit ourselves to lifelong learning.

The Church of the Nazarene's International Board of Education (IBOE) institutions remain one of the great treasures God has given the church. Currently we have a network of 50 colleges, universities, and seminaries providing education in 112 world areas. In addition, we have 1,023 learning centers run by our IBOE institutions, making it possible to reach out to many diverse locations. These institutions serve 43,476 students, not including daycares, primary schools, and secondary schools.[5]

Our respect for education is found on Scripture.

---

5. Church of the Nazarene, "Global Education," https://nazarene.org/index.php/iboe.

Colossians 1:16

For in him all things were created: things in heaven and on earth, visible and invisible, whether thrones or powers or rulers or authorities; all things have been created through him and for him."

This Colossians passage "magnificently celebrates Christ's sovereignty over all of creation and his supremacy over all powers. . . . Christ is truly Lord of heaven and earth."[6] All that we might study points us back to God. "For the Word of God was not made for us but rather we for him, and in him all things were created."[7] Laypersons in the Church of the Nazarene have historically been voracious learners. It was not uncommon for books on holiness to line the shelves of our laypeople's homes. The denominational magazine that is now known as *Holiness Today* was once found in the homes of most Nazarenes. Churches were planted by laypeople who only had the Bible and the magazine as their resource. Continual and ongoing education is part of our discipleship because it leads us into Christlikeness, which should always be the goal.

For those who attend public schools, education should be supplemented both in the church and the home. Early on, each church was encouraged to have Sunday school for every age group and to use a curriculum that would not only be age appropriate but was also designed to cover a progression of learning and needs over a period of time.

Theologians in the fourth century emphasized the importance of the Christian home and the nurture of children. One

---

6. Clinton E. Arnold, "Colossians," in *Romans to Philemon*, ed. Clinton E. Arnold, Zondervan Illustrated Bible Backgrounds Commentary: New Testament, Vol. 3 (Grand Rapids: Zondervan, 2002), 379.

7. Athanasius, *Discourses against the Arians* 2.18.31.

of the greatest theologians of all time, Gregory of Nazianzus, sometimes simply referred to as the Theologian, was raised in Cappadocia, in what is modern-day Turkey. His mother, Nonna, valued both secular and Christian education and invested in her children so they would be able to reach their highest educational potential.[8]

The Theologian's younger brother, Caesarius, was very bright, went on to study geometry and astronomy, and gained further education in Alexandria, Egypt, where he became a physician. Because of his great skill, Caesarius was given a number of positions in the Roman Empire, eventually becoming the first physician to Emperor Julian, who was known as the Apostate.[9] The emperor had been friends with the Theologian while studying at the university in Athens many years previous. While Caesarius was serving as the emperor's first physician, Julian challenged him to a debate over Christianity. The Theologian found this almost comical, for while Julian may have been emperor, Caesarius had been raised in Nonna's home! "Alas for this madness and folly if he hoped to take Caesarius, a man such as he was, my brother and the son of these parents, for his prey!"[10] It was no surprise to the Theologian that Caesarius won the debate, and he declared, "For victory is with Christ, who overcame the world."[11] For both the Theologian and Caesarius, the holy home provided much greater an

---

8. Nazianzen, *Epigr.* 142 (Paton, LCL). Referenced in Sunberg, *The Cappadocian Mothers*, 184.

9. Nazianzen, Or. 7.6 (PG 35:761-769) (SC 406) (FC, 4). Referenced in Sunberg, *The Cappadocian Mothers*, 184.

10. Nazianzen, Or. 7.6. Referenced in Sunberg, *The Cappadocian Mothers*, 184.

11. Nazianzen, Or. 7.6. Referenced in Sunberg, *The Cappadocian Mothers*, 184.

education than what the emperor had received. Christians have often been able to have significant influence for Christ while working in public institutions, although it may not be easy. For example, Caesarius had to flee for his life after winning his debate against the emperor.

In a practical sense, our commitment to education is also seen through our financial support of institutions and our participation on boards and committees. We encourage Nazarenes actively to support and engage in the educating and discipling of those who will come behind us. We participate in grace through education to be continually shaped and formed into Christlike disciples.

Questions for Reflection

1. Is your church providing lifelong discipleship education? If not, what could be done to fill in the gaps?

2. Why might it be important to support Christian higher education?

5
OFFER OUR WORK IN SACRIFICE TO GOD (¶28.7)

◆ 28.7. We call our people to remember that all our work is offered in service to God. As people fully committed to God, and uniquely gifted by Christ, the whole of each of our lives should fulfil God's purposes. All our work, paid or unpaid, should be done generously, ethically, and justly, in ways that promote the well-being of society and mirror Christlikeness.
(Gen. 12:1–3; Deut. 24:14–15; Eph. 4:28; Col. 3:22–25)

Work is a reflection of the covenantal relationship between God and humankind. God made a covenant with Abram, and in response, Abram was obedient. He left the place where he had been living and went into a new land. Abram's work was to live a life of obedience on a daily basis. He was to labor in the new land and would become a great nation there. This was God's side of the covenant promise. Abram's work was in response to the promise of God.

Genesis 12:1-3

The L*ord* *had said to Abram, "Go from your country, your people and your father's household to the land I will show you. I will* *make you into a great nation, and I will bless you; I will make your name great, and you will be a blessing. I will bless those who bless you, and whoever curses you I will curse; and all peoples on earth will be blessed through you."*

In the place where God sent him, Abram worked hard, and the result was blessing for him and for his family. Sacrificial labor is not done for the individual alone but for the entire community that ultimately reaps the benefits. Just as Christ would labor on the cross and give up his life sacrificially for the whole of humanity, so our labor is done for the benefit of those around us.

The covenant continues to be reflected in the relationship between the master and the day laborers. At times in our lives, we may find ourselves on either side of that relationship. If we find ourselves in the role of an employer, remember that we are to reflect Christ through the ways we respond to our employees. The justice of God should be seen in all our work.

Deuteronomy 24:14–15

Do not take advantage of a hired worker who is poor and needy, whether that worker is a fellow Israelite or a foreigner residing in one of your towns. Pay them their wages each day before sunset, because they are poor and are counting on it. Otherwise they may cry to the LORD against you, and you will be guilty of sin.

Delaying payment to an individual may result in needless hardship, and paying a migrant from another country less than we would pay a local worker is unjust. Fair treatment of workers is a "way of putting into practice the ideals of the covenant."[1] Our lives ought to be marked by paying a good and fair wage and by paying our debts on time. People should want to work for someone who is a Nazarene.

The way we perform our labor becomes a testimony to our walk with Jesus. Those who are wealthier, by "filling their obligations to their poor laborers, maintain the integrity of the community," reflecting the reality of God's covenant with humankind, which is why failure to "deal honestly in transactions of this sort brings severe condemnation."[2] At the same time, a strong work ethic also reflects the character of Christ. Not only should people want to work for someone who is a Nazarene, but a person or an organization should also want to hire a Nazarene.

Ephesians 4:28

Anyone who has been stealing must steal no longer, but must work, doing something useful with their own hands, that they may have something to share with those in need.

Work impacts the entire community. When an individual chooses not to work, or steals, they are not just impacting themselves but also all those around them. John Wesley calls this kind of stealing a sin and challenges Christlike disciples to do the opposite, inviting us in to ministering to others through our giving. Work provides us with the opportunity to share

---

1. Gordon McConville, *Deuteronomy*, ed. D. A Carson et al., New Bible Commentary: 21st Century Edition (Downers Grove, IL: InterVarsity Press, 1994), 221.
2. Peter C. Craigie, *The Book of Deuteronomy*, New International Commentary on the Old Testament (Grand Rapids: Eerdmans, 1976), 309.

with others and become life-giving, sustaining members of the community of faith.

Colossians 3:22–25

Slaves, obey your earthly masters in everything; and do it, not only when their eye is on you and to curry their favor, but with sincerity of heart and reverence for the Lord. Whatever you do, work at it with all your heart, as working for the Lord, not for human masters, since you know that you will receive an inheritance from the Lord as a reward. It is the Lord Christ you are serving. Anyone who does wrong will be repaid for their wrongs, and there is no favoritism.

This passage from Paul's letter to the church in Colossae brings up the relationship of slave and master. The language of slavery is troublesome, and this particular section of the household rules feels out of place in a world where ownership of one individual by another is repugnant. Yet Paul also writes this against the backdrop of Colossians 3:11: "Here there is no Gentile or Jew, circumcised or uncircumcised, barbarian, Scythian, slave or free, but Christ is all, and is in all." Paul has already stated that in Christ, they are part of a new community where all are free. Ambrosiaster, writing in the fourth century, comments: "Paul implies that God has created all persons to be freeborn and says this to keep masters from arrogance. Slavery is itself a sign of iniquity in the world, of the curse of Cain. In fact, the wise person is always free, though a slave outwardly, while it is foolish sinners who are the true slaves."[3]

---

3. Ambrosiaster, "Commentary on the Letter to the Colossians," in Peter Gorday and Thomas C. Oden, eds., *Colossians, 1–2 Thessalonians, 1–2*

Against this backdrop, Wesley suggests that no matter who we are, or our station in life, we have a different master, the Lord Jesus Christ, and we should be seeking to please him. "Menpleasers," he says, "are soon dejected and made angry: the single-hearted are never displeased or disappointed; because they have another aim, which the good or evil treatment of those they serve cannot disappoint."[4] Discipleship calls us to a Christian life in which we produce good works, not for salvation but that the purpose of new creation may be fulfilled in and through us. We are to participate in the good work of Christ because of the work of God that has been completed in Christ Jesus.[5] Let us work with a generous heart, and mirror Christlikeness in all that we do.

Questions for Reflection

1. What does a strong work ethic look like for a Christian?

2. What are some characteristics of a good employer?

3. What are some characteristics of a good employee?

Timothy, Titus, Philemon, Ancient Christian Commentary on Scripture, vol. 9 (Downers Grove, IL: InterVarsity Press, 2000), 53.

4. John Wesley, *Wesley's Notes on the Bible* (Altamonte Springs, FL: OakTree Software, 1997), ¶19446.

5. Bonhoeffer, *The Cost of Discipleship*, 296.

6
CAREFUL AND CONSIDERED USE OF MEDIA AND TECHNOLOGY (¶28.8)

◆ 28.8. We call our people to careful and considered use of media and technologies. We affirm the churches' use of technology in service to the kingdom, using it in a balanced way, prioritizing interpersonal relationships. Care must be taken to intentionally include those who have limited access. We must practice formation that helps people discern ways in which technologies may draw them away from engagement in actual community and family participation. We encourage disciples to live out the value of personal, face-to-face connection and to resist any form of living that would lead to isolation or create a culture of only virtual relationships, unless medically advised.
(Rom. 12:1; 1 Cor. 10:23–24; 2 Tim. 1:7)

The use of technology spread at a rapid rate during the COVID-19 pandemic. Even churches that thought they would never have an online presence, or electronic giving, found themselves adopting these alternatives in a relatively brief period of time. While technology has entered the church and is now a normal feature of ministry, it should never replace in-person connection.

SECTION I

When Paul wrote to the church in Rome, he encouraged them to think of their whole bodies as living sacrifices to be given over in true worship.

Romans 12:1

Therefore, I urge you, brothers and sisters, in view of God's mercy, to offer your bodies as a living sacrifice, holy and pleasing to God—this is your true and proper worship.

Technology provides the opportunity for people to worship from the safety and comfort of their home when needed, but it can also become tempting to stay home for good and no longer participate with the worshiping community. Lifting our voices in song, reading scriptures aloud, fellowshiping with one another, and partaking of the Lord's Supper happen when we gather together with God's people.

Beyond the bounds of worship, artificial intelligence (AI) is developing at such a rapid rate that it can easily become a two-edged sword. Brad Littlejohn, a PhD from the University of Edinburgh and a fellow in the Evangelicals and Civic Life program at the Ethics and Public Policy Center, warns us in regard to this developing technology:

> On the one hand, if well-conceived and well-used, it can help unlock hitherto unimagined human potential, allowing our minds and bodies to achieve extraordinary feats of creativity, power, and discovery, and steadily multiplying our capabilities. On the other hand, it can easily become anti-human, offering us pleasure or results without the trouble of thought or effort. Not only does the lack of effort take something away from the pleasure or achieve-

ment, but it deprives us of the opportunity for growth, causing our capabilities to atrophy.[1]

When writing to the church in Corinth, Paul notes that we have liberty in our Christian life, but this doesn't mean everything is good for us.

1 Corinthians 10:23–24

"I have the right to do anything," you say—but not everything is beneficial. "I have the right to do anything"—but not everything is constructive. No one should seek their own good, but the good of others.

As technology develops, we will have to pray for discernment regarding what is beneficial and constructive. Technology for technology's sake is not beneficial to the church unless it is constructive. The wide variety of tools available for discipleship are an example of the constructive, or edifying, ways we can use media to build up the Christian life. Providing online services to reach a community for Christ is constructive, as is reaching church members who are no longer able to leave their homes. Communicating through messaging apps, email, and other methods has made it easier to reach the whole church family and wider community. Social media can be used to reach people for Christ and to train in discipleship. Electronic meetings can also help bring people together and make the business of the church run smoothly, but these should never entirely replace getting together in the same space. Spending

---

1. Brad Littlejohn, "The Anti-human Temptation of AI," *World News Group*, August 8, 2024, https://wng.org/opinions/the-anti-human-temptation-of-ai-1723099543.

time with one another helps to strengthen relationships and bonds that build up the body of Christ.

People should not find themselves excluded from the church community because they do not have access to electronic tools. God can be glorified through technology, used in beautiful and creative ways, as long as the entire community has access. As a church community, we need to be discerning so that our use of technology does not become a stumbling block to a brother or sister.

When churches needed to transition to an online presence during the pandemic, many young people led the way in making it possible. This is a place where technology can bring us together. The intergenerational church family is brought together when one generation assists another.

Spending too much time on our devices has become a temptation in our modern world. The virtual world is no substitute for the real world that God created for us to enjoy. Minutes spent scrolling through social media can easily turn into hours. Artificial intelligence may soon encourage us to develop relationships with avatars, or individuals of our own creation. That is why the life of a disciple requires discipline.

2 Timothy 1:7

For the Spirit God gave us does not make us timid, but gives us power, love and self-discipline.

Through the power of the Spirit, we are able to cultivate the Christian life. It is essential that the church, as a community and a family, models a balanced approach to technology. Church leaders can lead by example, showing how technology can be used effectively without allowing it to control or overwhelm. Churches might encourage members to take periodic digital fasts or media breaks, helping them rediscover the value of simplicity, presence, and rest.

In a digital world, the call to careful and considered use of media and technology is both a responsibility and a blessing. Technology offers tools that can greatly benefit the church's ministry, outreach, and community-building efforts. However, it is the responsibility of believers to use these tools wisely, ensuring that our engagement with technology supports rather than undermines our faith, relationships, and participation in community. By prioritizing face-to-face relationships, fostering inclusivity, practicing discernment, and cultivating a healthy relationship with technology, the church can use these tools effectively in service to the kingdom. Through this approach, disciples are empowered to live out the values of personal connection, intentional living, and genuine community, offering a counter-cultural witness in a world that increasingly prioritizes the virtual over the real.[2]

Questions for Reflection

1. How can Christians model positive uses of technology in our lives?

2. What might you need to do in your own life or church community to create intentional space for face-to-face relationships?

---

2. This final paragraph was written by ChatGPT, an artificial intelligence program.

7
CARE FOR CREATION (¶28.9)

◆ 28.9. We call our people to care for creation. God pronounced the original creation to be good and appointed humanity to steward creation for God's greater purposes. Care for this created world includes such things as avoiding lifestyles of pollution and of unnecessary consumption of goods and resources.
(Gen. 1:26–28; John 1:3; Rom. 8:18–25; Col. 1:15–20)

The call to care for creation is deeply rooted in Scripture and aligns with God's original intent for humanity's role in the world. Humans are part of God's creation, members of God's ecosystem—along with all the other creatures. Therefore, we must find our place and live in harmony with all that God has created. In Isaiah, the praise of God is not limited to humans; even the trees of the field will clap their hands in praise. Too often we create division between humankind and nature, forgetting that we—as creatures ourselves—are part of nature as well.

Genesis 1:26–28 (NRSVUE)

Then God said, "Let us make humans in our image, according to our likeness, and let them have dominion over the fish of the sea and over the birds of the air and over the cattle and over all the wild animals of the earth and over every creeping thing that creeps upon the earth." So God created humans in his image, in the image of God he created them; male and female he created them. God blessed them, and God said to them, "Be fruitful and multiply and fill the earth and subdue it and have dominion over the fish of the sea and over the birds of the air and over every living thing that moves upon the earth."

Throughout the Bible, we see evidence that God values creation, and as stewards of the earth, humanity is appointed with the sacred responsibility to care for it, not only for its inherent goodness but also for God's greater purposes. This call to stewardship comes directly from the story of creation.

John's Gospel reveals Christ's role in creation.

John 1:3

Through him all things were made; without him nothing was made that has been made.

Combined, the creation narrative and the words from John challenge us to embrace God's creation and to recognize that humanity, created in the image of God, has been given a unique role in which we are to reflect God's authority and care for creation. Sadly, God's instructions to "rule over" and "subdue" the earth have often been misinterpreted as permission for unchecked exploitation. Yet, when seen through a broader biblical lens, we discover that the role is not one of unchecked power but of stewardship, in which our care of creation is actually an extension of God's love and creativity. This is another way in which a disciple may reflect the character of Christ.

Care for Creation

In the opening chapters of Genesis, we are invited into the garden of Eden. There, God is the gardener who carefully nurtures the plants, respects the health of the soil, and fosters an environment where life can flourish. As disciples, we are to follow this example and steward this earth so it remains healthy and capable of sustaining life. This task, entrusted to us by God, invites believers to take a holistic view of creation care, acknowledging our interconnectedness with the natural world and the privilege of working alongside God's purposes.

Romans 8:18–25 (NRSVUE)

I consider that the sufferings of this present time are not worth comparing with the glory about to be revealed to us. For the creation waits with eager longing for the revealing of the children of God, for the creation was subjected to futility, not of its own will, but by the will of the one who subjected it, in hope that the creation itself will be set free from its enslavement to decay and will obtain the freedom of the glory of the children of God. We know that the whole creation has been groaning together as it suffers together the pains of labor, and not only the creation, but we ourselves, who have the first fruits of the Spirit, groan inwardly while we wait for adoption, the redemption of our bodies. For in hope we were saved. Now hope that is seen is not hope, for who hopes for what one already sees? But if we hope for what we do not see, we wait for it with patience.

Colossians 1:15–20

The Son is the image of the invisible God, the firstborn over all creation. For in him all things were created: things in heaven and on earth, visible and invisible, whether thrones or powers or rulers or authorities; all things have been created through him and for him. He is before all things, and in him all things hold together. And he is the head of the body, the church; he is the beginning and the firstborn from among the dead, so that in everything he might have the supremacy. For God was pleased to have all his fullness dwell in him, and through him to reconcile to himself all things, whether things on earth or things in heaven, by making peace through his blood, shed on the cross.

These passages underscore the idea that creation is not just a backdrop for human life but an extension of God's will and presence, with Christ at the core. Since we are called to become Christlike disciples, and because Christ is at the center of creation, then caring for the earth is a matter of honoring Christ and his work, which means we have to look beyond creation as simply existing to be useful to humanity, or as a resource to be consumed, to the reality that creation exists for God's glory. What we do as kingdom citizens and people of the new creation has an impact on the entire ecosystem.

This Christ-centered view means we are people marked by a lifestyle that honors Christ's work and presence in the world around us. The primary responsibility of Christian stewardship is centered on the salvation of humanity—for others to come to know Christ, and in this, God's glory is revealed. At the same time, God is also glorified in restored creation. One only needs to spend a few quiet moments in the beauty of creation to experience the mystery of God's power. "Good stewardship of creation becomes the ability of human beings to manage all spiritual and material goods granted by God in order to glorify him."[1] As true stewards, we must remain keenly aware that everything we have comes from the Lord.

---

1. Angela Moreno, "A Criação De Deus, O Maior Desafio Do Século Xxi: Mudança Climática Ou A Má Mordomia?" Unpublished article, 19–20,

The reality is that we are witnessing "an ever-increasing and rapid overexploitation of natural resources in order to meet the growing needs for energy, food, transportation, education, health, materials for building and infrastructure, as well as for the production of an endless series of consumer goods and even superfluous luxuries," which has "created a civilization that is characterized by disrespect for nature, consumerism, unsustainability, and high levels of waste."[2] While God did give the earth and everything in it to humanity, it has been poorly managed over the centuries. This poor management reflects the change in humanity's relationship with God, which is why Paul's words written two thousand years ago still ring true—"all of creation is groaning." The mismanagement and abuse of creation are simply "sinful acts generated by the greed and wickedness of human beings."[3]

Even now, we are called to participate in the process of renewal, working toward the healing and restoration of creation, including advocating for practices that protect the earth and restore damaged environments. By participating in efforts that protect the vulnerable and promote restoration, believers can reflect God's love, providing a glimpse of the ultimate renewal that is to come. When the church understands its role from a Christ-centered perspective, we can help depoliticize environmental issues and break down the prejudice some people may have against Christians.

---

translation mine. Dr. Angela Moreno, PhD, is a widely revered environmental scientist, a member of the Church of the Nazarene in the Cape Verde Islands, and a member of the General Board of the Church of the Nazarene, representing the Africa Region.

2. Moreno, "*A Criação De Deus*," 20.
3. Moreno, "*A Criação De Deus*," 21.

At times, Christians are seen as those who do not care about the state of the environment. This view of Christianity can be altered when we embrace our role as stewards of all that God has created. Through our lifestyles, we become models of Christ and his care. Through active creation care, education, and sustainable practices, the church can model our desire to relieve the suffering state of humanity and creation. In this way, we reflect God's compassion and justice, inviting others to see his love in action. More than this, we become confessors that Christ is the healer of creation and the source of creation's eventual triumphant resolution.[4]

Ultimately, the call to care for creation is a sacred responsibility that aligns with God's original design and redemptive purposes. Through faithful stewardship of creation, believers can live out a gospel that is holistic, God-honoring, others-serving, and that cherishes the world he has entrusted to us.

Questions for Reflection

1. What are some examples of Christian stewardship of creation?

2. How have we mismanaged creation?

3. Why is it important for Christians to intentionally attend to caring for creation?

---

4. Moreno, "*A Criação De Deus*," 28–30.

8
BE PEACEMAKERS (¶28.10)

◆ 28.10. We call our people to be peacemakers. Because Jesus blessed peacemakers and commanded us to love our enemies, we commit ourselves to being agents of reconciliation in our families, among friends, at the workplace, in our churches, societies, nations, people groups, and tribes.
(Ps. 34:14; Matt. 5:9, 43–48; 2 Cor. 5:18–20; Eph. 2:14–16; Heb. 12:14)

In a polarized world, we are called to bring people together, united in God's love, and serve as peacemakers. Long ago the psalmist encouraged those who followed God to:

Psalm 34:14

Turn from evil and do good; seek peace and pursue it.

John Wesley said we are not to wait for peace to be offered, "but follow hard after it, when it seems to flee away from thee."[1] We are to be people who chase after peace, willing to put in the work it takes for peace to be realized in our midst.

---

1. Wesley, *Wesley's Notes on the Bible*, ¶8435.

SECTION I

As followers of Jesus, we reject expressions of violence and hatred and seek ways to be loving, forgiving, and charitable.

Matthew 5:9

Blessed are the peacemakers, for they will be called children of God.

This scripture is from Jesus's Sermon on the Mount. Shortly after praising those who make peace, Jesus continues by telling us we are called to be salt and light in our world: "In the same way, let your light shine before others, so that they may see your good works and give glory to your Father in heaven" (Matt. 5:16, NRSVUE). Like the Lord we follow, we are called to be peacemakers and to have a positive impact as salt and light in our world. We cannot do these things apart from God's grace, experienced in the power of the Holy Spirit.

As the Sermon on the Mount continues, Jesus expounds on what it means to be a peacemaker, and to love your neighbor.

Matthew 5:43–48

You have heard that it was said, "Love your neighbor and hate your enemy." But I tell you, love your enemies and pray for those who persecute you, that you may be children of your Father in heaven. He causes his sun to rise on the evil and the good, and sends rain on the righteous and the unrighteous. If you love those who love you, what reward will you get? Are not even the tax collectors doing that? And if you greet only your own people, what are you doing more than others? Do not even pagans do that? Be perfect, therefore, as your heavenly Father is perfect.

This language of perfection has been, from time to time, a challenge for the church; however, it is language that John Wesley embraced. He felt that every believer should seek Christian perfection, which was the term he used for his understanding of ethical holiness. In the Hebrew sense, the word translated "perfection" meant to fulfill the purpose for which something was created. Therefore, we come to understand that fulfilling the purpose for which we have been created as God's holy people includes becoming peacemakers. This is ethical holiness—reflecting, or mirroring, the peace of Jesus to the world. And this is what we were created to do from the very beginning. We become perfect when we fulfill what God has already prepared for us to do.

As a result, we are to become active agents of reconciliation.

2 Corinthians 5:18–20

All this is from God, who reconciled us to himself through Christ and gave us the ministry of reconciliation: that God was reconciling the world to himself in Christ, not counting people's sins against them. And he has committed to us the message of reconciliation. We are therefore Christ's ambassadors, as though God were making his appeal through us. We implore you on Christ's behalf: Be reconciled to God.

Our reconciliation with others becomes a reflection of our relationship with God. Those outside the church will find our testimony hard to accept if we cannot be a people of peace. If all of God's children actively engaged in chasing after peace, the world would be a different place. Even when we are under pressure to choose sides in the great divides of our day, God's people are to be actively engaged in bringing people together. This striving for peace and unity should especially be true in the life of the church, where Jesus declared that the world would know his disciples because of the way we love one another (John 13:35).

Our unity must be lived out in the life of the local church. Board meetings should not be a place where we fight battles to have things done our way, but should reflect the love of Jesus that brings people together. Our arguments over the color of the carpet or the church's priorities have not always reflected Jesus's peace and love. Peace seems to open a pathway for the Spirit to move in a church, but by the same token, when there is no peace, there is no Spirit. That is why holiness and peacemaking are so closely connected. Working for peace may require, at times, some real soul-searching as we determine a way forward. Living as agents of God's grace will stretch our faith and help us grow in our journey toward Christlikeness. The early church lived into this challenge, and Tertullian, writing in the second century, commented that the witness of the church had resulted in the world saying, "See how they love one another."[2]

We are called to be peacemakers not only within the church but also in relationships with those we encounter on a daily basis. As agents of peace and reconciliation, we should be the ones reaching out to bring healing to relationships in our families, among our friends, and in our workplaces. By doing this, we become channels of God's prevenient grace, reflecting the love of Jesus through our actions to those around us and helping to draw people toward Christ.

Becoming peacemakers in society may be tricky, yet we are compelled to be agents of God's love and peace, even among

---

2. Tertullian, *The Apology*, chapter 39.

those who do not get along. Years ago, the Church of the Nazarene developed a compassionate ministry center in the middle of Belfast, Northern Ireland. Both the city and the country had been torn apart by violence for decades. Neighborhoods painted their curbs to show whether they were Protestant or Catholic. Walls topped with razor wire divided communities, and one lived in fear of accidentally walking down the wrong street. Billy Mitchell was a Nazarene who had a vision to develop a cross-cultural conflict transformation ministry in Northern Ireland, which became known as LINC (Local Initiatives for Needy Communities). Mitchell created this ministry under the guidance and support of the church, which helped form a resource center. Under the auspices of Nazarene Compassionate Ministries, this center was dedicated to facilitating Christian compassion by reaching out to all sections of the community, developing conflict transformation initiatives in Belfast and surrounding areas to help embed a process for peace. These community initiatives continued following Mitchell's untimely death in 2006, playing a large role in creating a new generation of peace builders.

Throughout history, humans have identified with particular families, people groups, tribes, or nations. These identities have helped shape the world but at the same time have also created dividing lines. Just like the city of Belfast that was carved into sections by "peace walls," so we have created our own walls to determine who is in and who may be out. The early Christians struggled with the dividing walls between being a Jew and a gentile. The Jews considered themselves to be very religious while the gentiles were pagans. Yet Jesus came to be a peacemaker between such diverse groups of people so they could become one in him.

SECTION I

Ephesians 2:14–16

For he himself is our peace, who has made the two groups one and has destroyed the barrier, the dividing wall of hostility, by setting aside in his flesh the law with its commands and regulations. His purpose was to create in himself one new humanity out of the two, thus making peace, and in one body to reconcile both of them to God through the cross, by which he put to death their hostility.

Jesus becomes our model, and the church is to be a community in which there are no dividing walls. Members of the church are to be actively engaged in tearing down the walls that society may be creating.

Hebrews 12:14

Make every effort to live in peace with everyone and to be holy; without holiness no one will see the Lord.

Holiness and peacemaking go hand in hand. To be Christlike disciples means we are called to live as God's holy people in this world. Through our participation in Christ, we are made holy, creating the pathway for us to see the Lord. No wonder Wesley encouraged his followers to relentlessly pursue peace.

Questions for Reflection

1. When have Christians failed to be peacemakers in the world and in the church?

2. What kind of active effort does peacemaking involve?

3. How is peacemaking different from an absence of disagreement or conflict?

4. How could you and/or your church serve in a peacemaking role in your community?

SECTION II
We Are Called From . . .

9
THINGS THAT HINDER US (¶29)

◆ 29. As we search the Scriptures and develop discernment, we become aware of practices that do not promote the full potential of human beings. Such practices prevent the development of Christlikeness in believers and dishonor creation. Discernment calls us to "lay aside" those things that hinder us. We suggest that the standard given to John Wesley by his mother, Susanna, helps form a basis for the discernment of evil. She taught him, "Whatever weakens your reason, impairs the tenderness of your conscience, obscures your sense of God, or takes off the relish of spiritual things, whatever increases the authority of your body over mind, that thing for you is sin." Discernment regarding the things we lay aside forms part of our discipleship, accountability, and corporate witness. Growth in discipleship will increase our people's ability to discern harmful messages that encourage or glorify destruction, impurity, immorality, or violence, and to refuse to participate in them or in what promotes them. Therefore, we call our people to manifest the fruit of the Spirit in their lives as a witness to God's transforming and creative power over sin and death. In full awareness that sin takes new forms in each generation, often working in innovative and destructive ways, the above calls are not intended to be exhaustive, but representative of a way of life that is formed by the Spirit enabling us to become Christlike, to the glory of God the Father. These practices form part of our discipleship and pursuit of corporate Christlikeness, as we continue on a journey of grace.

(Eph. 4:22; Col. 3:9; Heb. 12:1)

No one likes the idea of denying themselves something they want, or that they may believe they deserve. The world encourages us to embrace the things that make us feel good and, in this way, to be true to ourselves. Unfortunately, this mindset is antithetical to what it means to be a follower of Christ. We read in Matthew 16:24–26, "Then Jesus said to his disciples, 'Whoever wants to be my disciple must deny themselves and take up their cross and follow me. For whoever wants to save their life will lose it, but whoever loses their life for me will find it. What good will it be for someone to gain the whole world, yet forfeit their soul? Or what can anyone give in exchange for their soul?'" Truly, it would be sad to gain everything the world has to offer yet ultimately lose it all—just for momentary satisfaction. The call to self-denial is not a punishment. Instead, it sets us free so we can be drawn into Christlikeness. Shedding habits and activities that have been weighing us down becomes life-giving.

Ephesians 4:22

You were taught, with regard to your former way of life, to put off your old self, which is being corrupted by its deceitful desires.

The great deception is that our habits and momentary pleasures will satisfy the desires of our heart. We will always be faced with temptations, but if we seek the face of the Lord and continue moving toward him, through the power of the Holy Spirit we can leave the old self behind.

First-century disciples spoke truth to one another and spurred one another on to leave their previous lives behind. The church community served as a place of accountability where people were encouraged to follow in the footsteps of Jesus.

Colossians 3:9

Do not lie to each other, since you have taken off your old self with its practices.

To become part of the Christian community was to begin walking in the Christian life. The concepts found on these pages are not new but have been around since the founding of the first-century church. For more than two thousand years, believers have wrestled with what the Christian life looks like in their world. Those who have gone before us have set a standard, and they are cheering on the next generation.

Hebrews 12:1

Therefore, since we are surrounded by such a great cloud of witnesses, let us throw off everything that hinders and the sin that so easily entangles. And let us run with perseverance the race marked out for us.

We are not alone on this Christian journey, and as we continue to grow in Christlikeness, we can see that we are surrounded by the previous generations. Through experience, those who have gone before know that sin can entangle us, and they want us to be able to run freely in this season of our lives. Those who founded the Church of the Nazarene believed they were called *to* certain practices and *away from* others so that they, and we, can reflect the character of Jesus the Nazarene.

SECTION II

Questions for Reflection

1. What kinds of practices, pleasures, or habits hinder your life of faith or your walk with God?

2. How do you guard against giving in to temptations toward earthly pleasures that don't build up Christlike character?

10
SUBVERSIVE ENTERTAINMENTS AND ACTIVITIES (¶29.1)

◆ 29.1. We call our people to wisdom in their use of time, money, and bodies. Entertainment and activities subversive of the Christian ethic that promote consumerism, self-centeredness, violence, sensuality, and treating others as objects rather than persons created in the image of God are to be avoided. Because we are living in a day of moral confusion in which we face the encroachment of evil into our thoughts and lives through the various avenues of print and digital media, it is essential that we observe safeguards to keep us from becoming secularized and worldly. We have an obligation to witness against whatever trivializes or blasphemes God, as well as such social evils as violence, sensuality, pornography, profanity, and the occult, as portrayed by and through the commercial entertainment industry in its many forms and to endeavor to bring about the demise of enterprises known to be the purveyors of this kind of entertainment. This would include the avoidance of all types of entertainment ventures and media productions that produce, promote, or feature the violent, the sensual, the pornographic, the profane, or the occultic, or which feature or glamorize the world's philosophy of secularism, sensualism, and materialism and undermine God's standard of holiness of heart and life. This includes all forms of dancing that detract from spiritual growth and break down proper moral inhibitions and reserve. We encourage the church to teach and respond in keeping with practices of personal holiness, including Sabbath-keeping, and to contribute to the creation of positive modes of entertainment, arts, and sports.

(Phil. 4:8–9; Col. 3:23; Rom. 14:7–13; 1 Cor. 10:31–33; Eph. 5:1–18; Phil. 4:8–9; 1 Pet. 1:13–17; 2 Pet. 1:3–11).

We have been gifted a finite number of hours in a day to give attention to the things around us. As a result, we need to determine the best ways to use the time we have been given, so we must be discerning about the type of entertainment we choose to consume. Entertainment is not neutral; it is a vehicle for transmitting ideas, values, and beliefs. For instance, many forms of entertainment glorify materialism, presenting happiness as attainable through the acquisition of wealth and possessions. Other types of entertainment celebrate sensuality and personal gratification, reducing human relationships to transactions that are devoid of the dignity inherent in individuals created in God's image. Much of the content that is readily available for us to consume overtly promotes ideologies that conflict with Christian teachings.

The apostle Paul provides a framework for discerning what is worthy of a Christian's time and attention.

Philippians 4:8–9

Finally, brothers and sisters, whatever is true, whatever is noble, whatever is right, whatever is pure, whatever is lovely, whatever is admirable—if anything is excellent or praiseworthy—think about such things. Whatever you have learned or received or heard from me, or seen in me—put it into practice. And the God of peace will be with you.

This exhortation encourages believers to engage with content that uplifts the soul, aligns with God's truth, and fosters spiritual growth. In contrast, subversive entertainment is designed to captivate the mind and heart in ways that lead away from God, often normalizing behaviors and attitudes that are contrary to his will.

Previous generations often asked their children whether they would be comfortable with Jesus finding them in a particular location or engaging in a certain activity. Many youth pastors have asked that question! The apostle Paul challenges us to be mindful and intentional about everything we do.

Colossians 3:23

Whatever you do, work at it with all your heart, as working for the Lord, not for human masters.

We are to be working for the Lord, not engaged in activities that are pushed upon us by the world. Consumer-driven entertainment—such as reality television, influencer culture, and advertisements—perpetuates the false narrative that human identity and value are derived from possessions and appearances. These messages subtly undermine the Christian understanding that true worth comes from being created in God's image and redeemed by his grace. As Christians, we are called to reject this lie and instead practice stewardship, using resources to glorify God and serve others rather than indulging in self-centered pursuits.

Video games, movies, and television shows that glorify violence desensitize individuals to human suffering and trivialize the sanctity of life. These forms of entertainment often promote conflict resolution through aggression, directly contradicting Christ's teaching to love one's enemies and to be agents of peace. If we are to be a holiness people, then a Christian ethic calls for engaging with media that fosters empathy, justice, and reconciliation, standing against the normalization of violence in popular culture.

The entertainment industry frequently exploits sensuality, portraying relationships through the lens of lust and objectification. This treatment not only dehumanizes individuals but also erodes moral inhibitions, making sin appear acceptable or even desirable. We are called to guard our hearts and minds, avoiding media that promotes immoral relationships or portrays individuals as objects for consumption.

Profanity and blasphemy are pervasive in modern entertainment, trivializing God's name and mocking Christian values. Humor often comes at the expense of sacred truths, dulling reverence for God's holiness and authority. Believers are tasked with honoring God in all we do, including our choice of words and the media we consume. The call to holiness includes rejecting content that treats God's name or character with contempt.

Media that glorifies the occult, witchcraft, or other spiritual practices that are contrary to biblical truth undermines God's sovereignty and opens the door to spiritual confusion. While these themes may seem harmless or fantastical, they desensitize individuals to real spiritual dangers and misrepresent the nature of God's power and authority. Scripture warns against engaging in practices that lead to spiritual deception. We must remain vigilant in discerning entertainment that aligns with the truth of God's Word.

Often, we are called upon to be prudent about our choices because of the impact our choices may have on others. Paul cautions the Roman Christians about this very thing.

Romans 14:7–13

For none of us lives for ourselves alone, and none of us dies for ourselves alone. If we live, we live for the Lord; and if we die, we die for the Lord. So, whether we live or die, we belong to the Lord. For this very reason, Christ died and returned to life so that he might be the Lord of both the dead and the living.

You, then, why do you judge your brother or sister? Or why do you treat them with contempt? For we will all stand before God's judgment seat. It is written: "'As surely as I live,' says the Lord, 'every knee will bow before me; every tongue will acknowledge God.'"

So then, each of us will give an account of ourselves to God.

Therefore let us stop passing judgment on one another. Instead, make up your mind not to put any stumbling block or obstacle in the way of a brother or sister.

While we may believe that we personally can perceive whether a particular entertainment is edifying, others within the faith community may not be able to. Sometimes adults fail to realize the impact of their decisions on the hearts and minds of innocent children. We choose to avoid certain kinds of entertainments and activities so our actions will not be a stumbling block to others.

Paul also reminded the Corinthian church that everything they took upon themselves to do was for the purpose of glorifying God, including all social activities.

SECTION II

1 Corinthians 10:31–33

So whether you eat or drink or whatever you do, do it all for the glory of God. Do not cause anyone to stumble, whether Jews, Greeks or the church of God—even as I try to please everyone in every way. For I am not seeking my own good but the good of many, so that they may be saved.

Glorifying God and seeking the good of others are worthy goals for our lives. They lead us back to the greatest commandments, to love God and to love our neighbor. All of these take us beyond ourselves and help us recognize that our lives and behaviors are to reflect Jesus. We are following Jesus on this journey of discipleship:

Ephesians 5:1–18

Follow God's example, therefore, as dearly loved children and walk in the way of love, just as Christ loved us and gave himself up for us as a fragrant offering and sacrifice to God.

But among you there must not be even a hint of sexual immorality, or of any kind of impurity, or of greed, because these are improper for God's holy people. Nor should there be obscenity, foolish talk or coarse joking, which are out of place, but rather thanksgiving. For of this you can be sure: No immoral, impure or greedy person—such a person is an idolater—has any inheritance in the kingdom of Christ and of God. Let no one deceive you with empty words, for because of such things God's wrath comes on those who are disobedient. Therefore do not be partners with them.

For you were once darkness, but now you are light in the Lord. Live as children of light (for the fruit of the light consists in all goodness, righteousness and truth) and find out what pleases the Lord. Have nothing to do with the fruitless deeds of darkness, but

Subversive Entertainments and Activities

rather expose them. It is shameful even to mention what the disobedient do in secret. But everything exposed by the light becomes visible—and everything that is illuminated becomes a light. This is why it is said: "Wake up, sleeper, rise from the dead, and Christ will shine on you."

Be very careful, then, how you live—not as unwise but as wise, making the most of every opportunity, because the days are evil. Therefore do not be foolish, but understand what the Lord's will is. Do not get drunk on wine, which leads to debauchery. Instead, be filled with the Spirit.

We must be careful how we live, and this caution includes adopting intentional safeguards. Before engaging with any form of media or entertainment, we should ask whether it aligns with biblical principles and whether it promotes godly virtues. Does this activity glorify what is noble, pure, and admirable? Our churches should engage in discussions about media consumption, social activities, and their impact, assisting our people to discern what is God-honoring and what is not. Practical boundaries will also help limit exposure to certain types of media, such as setting screen time restrictions and using content filters.

As salt and light in the world (Matt. 5:13–16), Christians have a responsibility to challenge cultural norms that trivialize or blaspheme God. This posture involves not only avoiding subversive entertainment but also actively opposing its influence. Practical steps may include advocacy or speaking out against media and entertainment that promotes harmful values, and encouraging others to adopt biblical standards. It is important to provide support for positive alternatives by investing time, money, and resources in creative endeavors that reflect God's truth and beauty. This may include supporting Christian filmmakers, artists, and musicians or participating in community-based initiatives that offer wholesome entertainment. Christians can be agents of transformation within the entertainment industry by creating content that reflects God's character and promotes the common good.

1 Peter 1:13-17

Therefore, with minds that are alert and fully sober, set your hope on the grace to be brought to you when Jesus Christ is revealed at his coming. As obedient children, do not conform to the evil desires you had when you lived in ignorance. But just as he who called you is holy, so be holy in all you do; for it is written: "Be holy, because I am holy." Since you call on a Father who judges each person's work impartially, live out your time as foreigners here in reverent fear.

Not surprisingly, the conversation returns to holiness—because the call to be God's holy people requires an ethical response. The entertainment choices we make are not trivial; they shape our hearts, influence our relationships, and reflect our witness to the world. But we do not have to try to live this way on our own. Through the power of the Holy Spirit, we are able to live the holy life.

2 Peter 1:3-11

His divine power has given us everything we need for a godly life through our knowledge of him who called us by his own glory and goodness. Through these he has given us his very great and precious promises, so that through them you may participate in the divine nature, having escaped the corruption in the world caused by evil desires.

For this very reason, make every effort to add to your faith goodness; and to goodness, knowledge; and to knowledge, self-control; and to self-control, perseverance; and to perseverance, godliness; and to godliness, mutual affection; and to mutual affection, love. For if you possess these qualities in increasing measure, they will keep you from being ineffective and unproductive in your knowledge of our Lord Jesus Christ. But whoever does not have them is nearsighted and blind, forgetting that they have been cleansed from their past sins.

Therefore, my brothers and sisters, make every effort to confirm your calling and election. For if you do these things, you will never stumble, and you will receive a rich welcome into the eternal kingdom of our Lord and Savior Jesus Christ.

By rejecting entertainment that subverts the Christian ethic and that promotes consumerism, sensuality, violence, and other worldly philosophies, we bear witness to the transformative power of God's grace. As partakers of the divine nature, we can escape the corruptive influences of this world, honor God, and contribute to a culture that reflects his kingdom on earth.

SECTION II

Questions for Reflection

1. What does it mean to practice self-discipline, and how might this be in contrast to what the world is telling us?

2. How might secular entertainment promote non-Christian concepts?

3. How is God's name treated with contempt in entertainment? How should we as Christians respond?

4. Why is it important to protect small children from certain forms of media and entertainment?

5. What are some practical steps that Christians can take in response to the entertainment industry?

11
UNHEALTHY HABITS (¶29.2)

◆ 29.2. We call our people to identify, prevent, and resist behaviors that lead to unhealthy habits or compulsive actions. Commitment to excellence and wellness requires us to resist habits of mind and life that could lead to addictions. This endeavor demands corporate and personal wisdom, discernment and truth speaking. Because these behaviors and habits may remain hidden, we encourage the church to develop means of accountability in areas of potential bondage. As Christians, we are called to resist all forms of compulsive actions, from the most pernicious to those culturally acceptable. Recognizing these vary from nation to nation, they may include food, sporting or fitness life, legal stimulants, cosmetic surgery, internet, or shopping. We also encourage the church community to seek solutions for and understanding of those caught up in addictions.
(Rom. 12:1–2; 1 Cor. 6:19–20)

In a world that often celebrates instant gratification and unbridled indulgence, the Christian call to intentional living is both countercultural and essential. John Wesley and the early Methodist societies had regular class and band meetings. In those settings, they were intentionally accountable before one another, confessing where they had been tempted in the previous week and whether they had been attending to all the means of grace made available to them. This is our heritage, encouraging us to live lives that are transformed by the renewal of our minds so that we may honor God in our bodies and actions.

Romans 12:1–2

Therefore, I urge you, brothers and sisters, in view of God's mercy, to offer your bodies as a living sacrifice, holy and pleasing to God—this is your true and proper worship. Do not conform to the pattern of this world, but be transformed by the renewing of your mind. Then you will be able to test and approve what God's will is—his good, pleasing and perfect will.

1 Corinthians 6:19–20

Do you not know that your bodies are temples of the Holy Spirit, who is in you, whom you have received from God? You are not your own; you were bought at a price. Therefore honor God with your bodies.

The Holy Spirit comes to dwell on earth within our fragile human bodies. We are both individually and corporately the temple of the Holy Spirit, which is why practicing our faith in community is vitally important. Together, we are to identify and resist behaviors that can lead to unhealthy habits, compulsive actions, and addictions. Such vigilance requires personal discipline, corporate accountability, and an unwavering commitment to spiritual and physical wellness.

Human nature is susceptible to patterns of behavior that may initially appear harmless but can evolve into compulsive habits that dominate and distort life. These habits often begin as responses to stress, boredom, or cultural pressures but can escalate into full-blown addictions. Whether culturally acceptable or socially stigmatized, unhealthy behaviors compromise our physical, mental, and spiritual health.

Addictions, broadly defined, are compulsive actions that override rational decision making and enslave individuals to harmful practices. While the term often is equated with substance abuse, it can encompass a wide range of behaviors, including:

Food and Eating Habits

Overeating, or using food as a coping mechanism, can lead to physical health issues and hinder emotional well-being. Conversely, an obsession with dieting and body image can result in eating disorders.

Sporting and Fitness Life

Although physical exercise is beneficial for our bodies, an obsession with fitness or sports can lead to the neglect of other responsibilities and foster an idolatry of physical appearance or performance.

Legal Stimulants

The excessive use of substances like caffeine, nicotine, or energy drinks can develop into dependency, affecting health and decision making. At the same time, some parts of the world are legalizing the use of certain recreational drugs, challenging the Christian commitment to healthy habits in a changing landscape. It is important to understand that recreational drug use is defined as "the nonmedical use of psychoactive substances for the purpose of creating an altered state of consciousness (either to create pleasurable experiences or to escape unpleasantness)."[1] Ultimately, "what constitutes recreational drug use is determined by the intent of the use of a psychoactive drug rather than the legal status of the substance."[2]

Discussions surrounding the legality of recreational drugs should not dominate the conversation. What should drive the conversation is the call to a holy life—to be alert and sober, ready for the Lord's return. First Thessalonians 5:1–8 can guide our thinking on this matter:

> Now, brothers and sisters, about times and dates we do not need to write to you, for you know very well that the day of the Lord will come like a thief in the night. While people are saying, "Peace and safety," destruction will come on them suddenly, as labor pains on a pregnant woman, and they will not escape.
>
> But you, brothers and sisters, are not in darkness so that this day should surprise you like a thief. You are all children of the light and children of the day. We do not belong to the night or to the darkness. So then, let us not be like others, who are asleep, but let us be awake and sober. For those who sleep, sleep at night, and those who get drunk, get drunk at night. But since we belong to the day, let us be sober, putting on faith and love as a breastplate, and the hope of salvation as a helmet.

Cosmetic Surgery

Driven by societal standards of beauty, compulsive cosmetic procedures can reveal an unhealthy fixation on physical

---

1. Craig K. Svensson, *Recreational Drug Use: A Biblical Perspective* (Greensboro, NC: New Growth Press, 2023), 5.
2. Svensson, *Recreational Drug Use*, 5.

appearance, and they can also mask deeper insecurities. At its very core, a preoccupation with appearance is an unhealthy fixation with perfection, driving one to see the self as inherently inadequate and demonstrating a misunderstanding of Christian perfection.

Internet and Technology

The pervasive use of smartphones, social media, and streaming services often leads to compulsive behavior, eroding personal relationships, productivity, and spiritual disciplines.

Shopping and Consumerism

Retail therapy or compulsive buying fosters materialism, distracts from spiritual priorities, and can lead to financial strain.

Each of these behaviors, though they are all culturally normalized in varying degrees, has the potential to lead to spiritual and physical bondage. The good news is that Christians are called to live in freedom, not as slaves to destructive habits or cultural pressures. We don't conform to the habits of this world, but we are transformed. This transformation begins with recognizing the subtle ways that behaviors and habits can lead to bondage. It involves resisting the pull of compulsive actions, no matter how socially acceptable they may appear, and instead aligning every aspect of life with God's will.

The presence of a healthy church community becomes vital in helping to grow in grace. Avoiding unhealthy behaviors requires both personal discipline and the wisdom of a supportive community. Each member of the church community should be encouraged to cultivate habits of self-examination, prayer, and reflection to identify areas of vulnerability in their own lives.

On the personal level, a disciple should regularly seek the Lord's guidance through prayer, asking God to identify behaviors that may be developing into unhealthy habits. Immersion in Scripture can help provide clarity on God's standards and offer strength to resist temptation. At the same time, setting healthy boundaries on screen time, food consumption, and shopping can help prevent compulsive behaviors from taking root.

Some churches have formal support systems in place, but for those who do not, cultivating spaces for honest conversations about struggles and habits will help foster transparency and mutual support. Trusted accountability partners can provide encouragement, correction, and prayer to stay on track. Seasoned believers can mentor and disciple others in developing healthy habits and overcoming potential areas of bondage.

It is important to create a safe environment where all feel welcome without judgment so that people can seek help without fear. Local churches may provide workshops, counseling, and recovery programs to address specific challenges. Through sermons, Bible studies, and community events, church leaders can highlight the dangers of compulsive behavior and equip members with practical tools for resisting temptation. Finally, churches can partner with local organizations to address the systemic issues that contribute to addiction, such as poverty, unemployment, and lack of access to healthcare.

Unhealthy behaviors vary across cultural and national contexts. What may be a common struggle in one culture might not exist in another. For instance, Western cultures often grapple with materialism and digital addiction while other societies might face issues related to communal obligations or traditional practices. This diversity calls for a nuanced approach to identifying and addressing unhealthy behaviors, always guided by biblical principles rather than cultural norms.

Questions for Reflection

1. What are examples of harmful habits? What makes them harmful?

2. Why is community accountability in regard to habits or behaviors important?

3. What does self-sacrifice look like in your own life?

12
ALCOHOL AND OTHER INTOXICATING SUBSTANCES (¶29.3–29.4)

◆ 29.3. We call our people to abstain from drinking alcohol, thereby witnessing to the world. From its earliest days, Nazarenes refrained from drinking alcohol, as a witness to transformed lives. Because of the prevalence of alcohol abuse in our world, we ask our people to refrain from alcohol and other intoxicating substances as an expression of self-giving love and solidarity with individuals, families, and communities who suffer pain and trauma because of alcohol abuse and addiction. We recognize that other Christian traditions may respond to these issues differently. Nazarenes choose to abstain in response to the biblical mandate to love others. We welcome into our congregations those who are struggling with alcohol or other addictions, and in our welcome, we willingly abstain to make our faith community an environment of safety. Our position must be embodied with grace.
 (Lev. 19:18, 34; Prov. 20:1; 23:21; Mark 12:28–34; Rom. 13:8–10; 14:13–23; 1 Cor. 5:11; 6:10; Eph. 5:18; Phil. 2:4)

◆ 29.4. We call our people to abstain from intoxicants, tobacco, stimulants, depressants, and hallucinogens outside proper medical care and guidance, regardless of the legality and availability of such substances. Medical evidence demonstrates that these substances, when used outside of proper medical care and guidance, can be destructive, not just of the body, but of the mind, as well as families, social structures, and communities.

(1 Cor. 6:19–20)

Throughout its history, the Church of the Nazarene has upheld a commitment to abstain from alcohol as a testimony to the transformative power of Christ's love and grace. This stance is not merely a personal choice or legalistic rule but a compassionate response to the pervasive harm caused by alcohol abuse in society. In an era when alcohol is widely accepted and often celebrated, the Nazarene call to abstinence serves as a countercultural witness of self-giving love, solidarity, and holistic well-being. Grounded in biblical principles and shaped by a desire to create safe, grace-filled communities, this position underscores the importance of sacrificial love, accountability, and the pursuit of a life that reflects Christ's character.

God's people have always been asked to live sacrificially and to love our neighbors, whether those in our own community, or others whom God brings into our midst. When we consider those whom God wants us to invite into our communities, we choose to love first and foremost. In the early days of the first Church of the Nazarene in Los Angeles, ministry included outreach to the poor and to those who struggled with addiction and alcoholism. We are compelled by God's commands:

Leviticus 19:18, 34

Do not seek revenge or bear a grudge against anyone among your people, but love your neighbor as yourself. I am the Lord.

The foreigner residing among you must be treated as your native-born. Love them as yourself, for you were foreigners in Egypt. I am the LORD your God.

Many of those who were part of the early Holiness Movement that became part of the Church of the Nazarene were immigrants, coming to the United States from around the world. They made up the church, so the call to love reached beyond people groups or social barriers. Jesus reiterated this command and revealed that loving others had a great deal to do with participation in the kingdom of God.

Mark 12:28-34

One of the teachers of the law came and heard them debating. Noticing that Jesus had given them a good answer, he asked him, "Of all the commandments, which is the most important?"

"The most important one," answered Jesus, "is this: 'Hear, O Israel: The Lord our God, the Lord is one. Love the Lord your God with all your heart and with all your soul and with all your mind and with all your strength. The second is this: 'Love your neighbor as yourself.' There is no commandment greater than these."

"Well said, teacher," the man replied. "You are right in saying that God is one and there is no other but him. To love him with all your heart, with all your understanding and with all your strength, and to love your neighbor as yourself is more important than all burnt offerings and sacrifices."

When Jesus saw that he had answered wisely, he said to him, "You are not far from the kingdom of God." And from then on no one dared ask him any more questions.

SECTION II

The biblical command to love one's neighbor as oneself is central to the Nazarene position on abstinence. Paul's letter to the church in Rome encourages believers to avoid causing others to stumble by exercising their freedom in ways that might harm those who are vulnerable.

Romans 14:13–23

Therefore let us stop passing judgment on one another. Instead, make up your mind not to put any stumbling block or obstacle in the way of a brother or sister. I am convinced, being fully persuaded in the Lord Jesus, that nothing is unclean in itself. But if anyone regards something as unclean, then for that person it is unclean. If your brother or sister is distressed because of what you eat, you are no longer acting in love. Do not by your eating destroy someone for whom Christ died. Therefore do not let what you know is good be spoken of as evil. For the kingdom of God is not a matter of eating and drinking, but of righteousness, peace and joy in the Holy Spirit, because anyone who serves Christ in this way is pleasing to God and receives human approval.

Let us therefore make every effort to do what leads to peace and to mutual edification. Do not destroy the work of God for the sake of food. All food is clean, but it is wrong for a person to eat anything that causes someone else to stumble. It is better not to eat meat or drink wine or to do anything else that will cause your brother or sister to fall.

So whatever you believe about these things keep between yourself and God. Blessed is the one who does not condemn himself by what he approves. But whoever has doubts is condemned if they eat, because their eating is not from faith; and everything that does not come from faith is sin.

Abstaining from alcohol is an act of love that helps us to stand in solidarity with those who struggle with addiction. It is a commitment to ensuring that the faith community remains a place of safety and support for all. Scripture provides both direct and implicit guidance on the dangers of alcohol and the virtues of self-control, wisdom, and love. While the Bible does not universally condemn alcohol consumption, it does offer clear warnings about its potential to impair judgment, cause harm, and lead to sinful behavior. Proverbs provides stark warnings about the consequences of drunkenness.

Proverbs 20:1

Wine is a mocker and beer a brawler; whoever is led astray by them is not wise.

Proverbs 23:21

For drunkards and gluttons become poor, and drowsiness clothes them in rags.

Here we find a vivid picture of the destructive effects of excessive drinking, highlighting the physical, emotional, and spiritual toll it can take. These warnings emphasize the potential for alcohol to enslave individuals, impair their ability to make wise choices, and cause relational harm.

Paul's exhortation to the church in Ephesus further reinforces the call to abstain.

Ephesians 5:18

Do not get drunk on wine, which leads to debauchery. Instead, be filled with the Spirit.

The contrast between being controlled by alcohol and being filled with the Holy Spirit underscores the Christian calling to pursue holiness and self-control. Abstaining from alcohol serves as a tangible expression of living a Spirit-filled life, characterized by discipline, clarity of mind, and a focus on God's purposes.

The decision to abstain from alcohol serves as a public declaration that believers have been set apart for God's purposes. It demonstrates a break from the patterns of the world (Rom. 12:2) and a commitment to embody the values of God's kingdom. In communities where alcohol abuse is prevalent, this countercultural choice serves as a beacon of hope, signaling that freedom from addiction is possible through the power of Christ.

Alcohol abuse is a pervasive issue, causing immense harm to individuals, families, and communities. In the United States, approximately 23.5 percent of individuals may binge drink in a given month.[1] This is nearly a quarter of the adult population. By choosing to abstain, Nazarenes express solidarity with those who have been affected by the pain and trauma of addiction. This act of self-denial is a tangible expression of Christ's command to bear one another's burdens (Gal. 6:2) and prioritize the well-being of others over our own personal freedoms.

---

1. Substance Abuse and Mental Health Services Administration (SAMHSA), "National Survey on Drug Use and Health," July 30, 2024, https://www.samhsa.gov/data/data-we-collect/nsduh-national-survey-drug-use-and-health. See Table 2.28A, https://www.samhsa.gov/data/report/2023-nsduh-detailed-tables.

Romans 13:8-10

Let no debt remain outstanding, except the continuing debt to love one another, for whoever loves others has fulfilled the law. The commandments, "You shall not commit adultery," "You shall not murder," "You shall not steal," "You shall not covet," and whatever other command there may be, are summed up in this one command: "Love your neighbor as yourself." Love does no harm to a neighbor. Therefore love is the fulfillment of the law.

Western society has a long history of alcohol consumption, primarily related to poor drinking water. It was not until the nineteenth century, with the discovery of microorganisms and the advent of filtration systems, that clean water became available to much of the world's population. That is why Western society became accustomed to drinking beer and wine, while in the far East people boiled water for tea for their hydration. Bear in mind, the original forms of beer and wine were much lower in alcohol content, undergoing a natural and organic fermentation process that reduced harmful microorganisms. A process of distillation was developed around 1100, which greatly increased the percentage of alcohol in both beer and wine. This stronger form of drink gained popularity in western Europe around the fifteenth century, just as the world was dealing with the Black Plague. It may have been an emotional way to cope with the plague, but Europeans began drinking more of the distilled products with a greater concentration of alcohol.[2]

---

2. Bert L. Vallee, "The Conflicted History of Alcohol in Western Civilization," June 1, 2015, https://www.scientificamerican.com/article/the-conflicted-history-of-alcohol-in-western-civilization/.

SECTION II

The result was devastating. People were unable to maintain safe limits of consumption, and many became addicted.[3] In the early nineteenth century, more scientific principles informed the practice of medicine and allowed "clinical symptoms to be categorized into diseases that might then be understood on a rational basis,"[4] which led to the study of alcohol abuse by two scientists, one from the UK and the other from the U.S. In their 1813 essay on drunkenness, they described "alcohol abuse as a disease and recognized that habitual and prolonged consumption of hard liquor causes liver disease, accompanied by jaundice, wasting and mental dysfunction, evident even when the patient is sober."[5]

The Methodist movement at the time was strongly anti-alcohol and greatly concerned with the impact of alcohol consumption on society.[6] This movement was the impetus for the study by the two scientists, which resulted in an understanding of the pathology of alcohol abuse. It remains one of the most important health problems facing the world today. In the United States, abuse of alcohol is one of the top ten risk factors for poor health and is a major agent of disruption in people's lives and relationships with others.[7] From its inception, the Church of the Nazarene has emphasized the importance of living a life that visibly reflects the transforming power of Christ. Abstaining from alcohol is a powerful witness to the world, signaling

---

3. Mary-Anne Enoch, "Genetic Influences on the Development of Alcoholism," *Current Psychiatry Reports*, vol. 15, no. 412 (2013) https://pmc.ncbi.nlm.nih.gov/articles/PMC4159132/.
4. Vallee, "The Conflicted History."
5. Vallee, "The Conflicted History."
6. Vallee, "The Conflicted History."
7. Vallee, "The Conflicted History."

that the people of God are called to a higher standard of living marked by purity, compassion, and self-sacrifice.

The church is called to be a refuge for those who are struggling, a place where individuals can experience grace, healing, and transformation. Abstaining from alcohol plays a crucial role in fostering an environment of safety and support. For individuals recovering from addiction, the presence of alcohol in social settings can be a source of temptation and anxiety. By choosing to abstain, the faith community ensures that church gatherings, events, and fellowship opportunities are free from this potential stumbling block, creating a safe space for all to participate without fear.

While the call to abstain is clear, it must be embodied with grace. The church must avoid judgmental attitudes and instead offer a welcoming embrace to those who struggle with alcohol addiction. This approach reflects the heart of Christ, who extended compassion to the broken and invited them into a transformative relationship with him. The church also plays a vital role in supporting individuals on the journey to recovery, including providing resources such as counseling, support groups, and mentorship, as well as fostering an environment of accountability where individuals can be honest about their struggles and receive encouragement. The implications for abstinence are far reaching, both for the church and broader society. Abstaining from alcohol contributes to overall physical and mental health. By choosing to abstain, believers prioritize their well-being and model a lifestyle that promotes health and vitality. It serves as a prophetic witness to the value of self-control, the importance of community, and the transformative power of love.

SECTION II

Alcohol abuse is a contributing factor to numerous social issues, including domestic violence, poverty, and crime. By abstaining, the church takes a stand against these injustices and demonstrates a commitment to social responsibility. This stance also provides a platform for advocating for policies and practices that address the root causes of addiction and support those in recovery.

The apostle Paul was concerned about the witness and testimony of the Christian community. While God's people are to serve as a community of grace, those who actively bear the name "Christian" are to follow after Jesus and reflect his character. The world can see through the hypocrisy of the church, and that is why Paul was adamant about those who claimed to be Christ followers living out their lives in an ethical manner.

1 Corinthians 5:11; 6:10

But now I am writing to you that you must not associate with anyone who claims to be a brother or sister but is sexually immoral or greedy, an idolater or slanderer, a drunkard or swindler. Do not even eat with such people.

. . . nor thieves nor the greedy nor drunkards nor slanderers nor swindlers will inherit the kingdom of God.

The issue here is someone "who claims to be a brother or sister" in Christ. Great damage can be done to the witness of the church when someone claims to be a believer but lives a lifestyle that does not reflect Christ. The church board member who is caught drunk driving becomes a poor reflection on the entire Christian community. This is why Paul saved his harshest words for those within the church.

Philippians 2:4

. . . not looking to your own interests but each of you to the interests of the others.

As Christians we are not only supposed to consider what might be lawful but also what may build up others, both inside and outside the Christian community. Throughout Christian history, we are warned not to use our own liberty to make ourselves feel good, but in all we do—eating, drinking, fellowshipping—our aim should be to glorify God.

Ephesians 5:15–20

Be very careful, then, how you live—not as unwise but as wise, making the most of every opportunity, because the days are evil. Therefore do not be foolish, but understand what the Lord's will is. Do not get drunk on wine, which leads to debauchery. Instead, be filled with the Spirit, speaking to one another with psalms, hymns, and songs from the Spirit. Sing and make music from your heart to the Lord, always giving thanks to God the Father for everything, in the name of our Lord Jesus Christ.

This admonition from the apostle Paul is relevant both to alcohol and to the use and abuse of other substances. In Paul's letter to the Ephesians, he is encouraging disciples to become imitators of Christ, all within the context of a culture that is at odds with the life of a Christian. God's people are to be new creation, and if this is true, then there is also new living. In Ephesians, people were familiar with the worship of Greek and Roman gods. The people who worshiped Dionysius would drink until they were drunk as part of their ritual. When they were filled with the wine and acted in odd ways, they believed it was a sign of being filled with the spirit of Dionysius. Therefore, drunkenness was associated with god worship. Drunkenness plagued the culture in Ephesus, which is why Paul contrasts the use of wine with the infilling of the Spirit. It is a challenge to those who believed they needed wine to lift their spirits, rather than depending on the filling of the Holy Spirit.

The fifth-century church father John Chrysostom put it this way:

> Be ready for the Spirit's filling. This happens only when we have cleansed our souls of falsehood, anger, bitterness, sexual impurity, uncleanness and covetousness. It happens only when we have become compassionate, meek and forgiving to one another, only when facetiousness is absent, only when we have made ourselves worthy. Only then does the Spirit come to settle within our hearts, only when nothing is there to prevent it. Then he will not only enter but also fill us.[8]

Therefore, when we are tired and weary, anxious and afraid, we should not seek to have our spirits lifted by the drinking of alcohol or the use of other drugs. In the end, abusing drugs and alcohol can make us feel even more sorrowful. Instead, through prayer and singing the psalms, we are to seek to be filled with the Holy Spirit. In this way, we can avoid those things that may keep us from living as new creations.

Chrysostom's message on this passage is powerful, so we continue:

> Do you wish to be happy? Do you want to know how to spend the day truly blessed? I offer you a drink that is spiritual. This is not a drink for drunkenness that would

---

8. John Chrysostom, "Homily On Ephesians," 19.5.19–21.

cut off even meaningful speech. This does not cause us to babble. It does not disturb our vision. Here it is: Learn to sing psalms! Then you will see pleasure indeed. Those who have learned to sing with the psalms are easily filled with the Holy Spirit. But if you sing only the devil's songs you will soon find yourself filled with an unclean spirit.[9]

New creation means new living, day in and day out, focused on giving thanks to God, our lives an offering in worship before our Lord.

Society has, at times, legalized products that remain harmful to our bodies and minds. Today, depending on the country, a variety of potentially harmful products are legally available, and the impact on communities is only beginning to be seen. At times, people have chided the church for being behind the times, when in reality, the call to abstain from certain substances has ultimately been embraced by society. Early on, the church called people to avoid smoking tobacco products, and today nearly all nations of the world provide warnings to their citizens regarding the harmful impact of smoking.[10] The newest addition is e-cigarettes, which also contain the addictive substance nicotine, as well as other harmful components.[11]

---

9. Chrysostom, "Homily On Ephesians," 19.5.19–21.

10. U.S. National Library of Medicine, "The Health Consequences of Smoking—50 Years of Progress: A Report of the Surgeon General: Fifty Years of Change, 1964–2014," https://www.ncbi.nlm.nih.gov/books/NBK294310/. This report gives an update on the impact of the 1964 report that outlined the health problems created by smoking and the subsequent changes in society.

11. The U.S. Centers for Disease Control, Smoking and Tobacco Use: Health Effects of Vaping, May 15, 2024, https://www.cdc.gov/tobacco/e-cigarettes/health-effects.html.

A number of countries have legalized marijuana, which raises new questions. A variety of new smokable and edible products have become legally available. The long-term impact of these changes is just beginning to be seen. Just as society encouraged cigarette smoking for the first half of the twentieth century but then saw the dangers, the same is beginning to play out regarding the legalization of these products, especially the impact on young people. Because of legalization, there has been a

> decrease in perceived harmfulness of the drug and an increase in its use among youth. This change is of critical concern because of the potential harmful impact of marijuana exposure on adolescents. Marijuana use has been associated with several adverse mental health outcomes, including increased incidence of addiction and comorbid substance use, suicidality, and new-onset psychosis. Negative impacts on cognition and academic performance have also been observed.[12]

1 Corinthians 6:19–20

Do you not know that your bodies are temples of the Holy Spirit, who is in you, whom you have received from God? You are not your own; you were bought at a price. Therefore honor God with your bodies.

---

12. Kristie Ladegard, Christian Thurstone, and Melanie Rylander, "Marijuana Legalization and Youth," *Pediatrics* Vol 145, Supplement 2 (May 2020): S165–S174, https://publications.aap.org/pediatrics/article-abstract/145/Supplement_2/S165/34451/Marijuana-Legalization-and-Youth?redirectedFrom=fulltext?autologincheck=redirected.

In a culture that often glorifies alcohol consumption and the use of intoxicants, tobacco, stimulants, depressants, and hallucinogens of all kinds, the decision to abstain serves as a powerful countercultural statement. It challenges societal norms and invites others to consider the impact of their choices on themselves and their communities. In a world marred by the destructive effects of substance abuse, the Nazarene stance on abstinence is a compelling testament to the power of grace, love, and the transformative work of Christ.

Questions for Reflection

1. How can abstinence from alcohol reflect the character of Christ?

2. Which biblical command is central to understanding our position on alcohol?

3. How should we respond to the legalization of products that can be harmful?

13
GREED (¶29.5)

◆ 29.5. We call our people to resist greed in all forms. It is vital that we reject all acts of greed that promote wealth over wellness or status over humility. We do not support distorted, biblically unsound messages about prosperity. Economic practices that oppress and take advantage of others are to be avoided. Schemes such as lotteries, legal or illegal gambling, payday loan organizations, pyramid schemes, often take needed financial resources from the poor and elderly with false promises of return.
(Eph. 4:28; 2 Thess. 3:6–13)

Greed, at its core, is an excessive desire for more than what is needed or deserved—whether wealth, food, possessions, or power. This constant desire for more can foster anxiety and a sense of emptiness, and it blinds people to the true sources of joy: relationships with God and others. Greed is not merely a private sin but a force that can have far-reaching consequences for families, communities, and societies, ultimately resulting in systemic injustice and exploitation.

Economic practices that are driven by greed—such as payday loans, gambling, and pyramid schemes—prey on the vulnerable, particularly the poor and elderly, promising quick wealth but delivering hardship and debt. These schemes exacerbate inequality, trapping individuals in cycles of poverty and despair.

New creation humanity chooses to mirror the truth patterned in the life of Christ. When one engages in greed, they are essentially stealing from others and destroying trust within the community. This was of such a concern to Paul that he addressed it in the letter to the Ephesians.

Ephesians 4:28

Anyone who has been stealing must steal no longer, but must work, doing something useful with their own hands, that they may have something to share with those in need.

Essentially, greed corrupts a person's moral character by promoting selfishness over selflessness and dishonesty over integrity. It leads individuals to value wealth and status above compassion, humility, and fairness, creating a community where the strong exploit the weak and the pursuit of profit is of more value than ethical considerations.

In the fourth century, the church leader Basil of Caesarea wrote to the wealthy within his church:

> You gorgeously array your walls, but do not clothe your fellow human being; you adorn horses, but turn away from the shameful plight of your brother or sister; you allow grain to rot in your barns, but do not feed those who are starving; you hide gold in the earth but ignore the oppressed! And if your wife happens to be a money-loving person, then the disease is doubled in its effects.[1]

---

1. Basil, Homily 7, "To the Rich," 4.47.

Basil's words were a warning that the witness of the church was being tarnished by the actions of those in the church community. From the earliest days of Christianity, disciples have been implored to work hard and to be generous both to those in the church community and beyond. John Wesley, in his sermon "The Use of Money," famously said, "gain all you can," "save all you can," and "give all you can."[2]

The preaching from Wesley is in direct opposition to what is known as "prosperity gospel" theology, or sometimes it's called "health and wealth" preaching. This is a religious belief that wealth comes as a divine reward for a person's faith in God. Prosperity preaching is based on a transactional model with a focus on receiving material wealth. Sadly, the teaching blames individuals' lack of faith for any misfortunes in life. Additionally, this teaching may be used to financially exploit the poor and the emotionally vulnerable. The following warning comes to us from South Africa: "When the gospel is used to manipulate and to support the self-aggrandizement and material enrichment of so-called pastors who are peddlers of their own personality cults rather than purveyors of the good news about Jesus, this should be firmly rebuked and repudiated as heretical and anti-Christian."[3]

---

2. John Wesley, "Sermon 50: The Use of Money," Wesley Center Online, https://wesley.nnu.edu/john-wesley/the-sermons-of-john-wesley-1872-edition/sermon-50-the-use-of-money/.

3. Joshua Robert Barron, "Is the Prosperity Gospel, Gospel? An Examination of the Prosperity and Productivity Gospels in African Christianity," *Conspectus: The Journal of the South African Theological Seminary* 33:11 (April 2022), 88–103, https://journals.co.za/doi/epdf/10.54725/conspectus.2022.1.6.

SECTION II

To avoid greed and distorted views of the gospel, God's people are to be hard workers. The apostle Paul was concerned about the work ethic among the church folks in Thessalonica.

2 Thessalonians 3:6–13

In the name of the Lord Jesus Christ, we command you, brothers and sisters, to keep away from every believer who is idle and disruptive and does not live according to the teaching you received from us. For you yourselves know how you ought to follow our example. We were not idle when we were with you, nor did we eat anyone's food without paying for it. On the contrary, we worked night and day, laboring and toiling so that we would not be a burden to any of you. We did this, not because we do not have the right to such help, but in order to offer ourselves as a model for you to imitate. For even when we were with you, we gave you this rule: "The one who is unwilling to work shall not eat."

We hear that some among you are idle and disruptive. They are not busy; they are busybodies. Such people we command and urge in the Lord Jesus Christ to settle down and earn the food they eat. And as for you, brothers and sisters, never tire of doing what is good.

Here we find practical advice, urging people to be neither greedy nor slothful. To be part of the church community meant you were to take responsibility for your personal life, and that meant working hard. Those who were able to work were to do everything they could to be busy with their hands. A disciple was to practice self-discipline, not making a big deal about their work but simply going about their business and not tiring of doing the right thing.

Nazarenes have a history of being generous givers and regular tithers. We encourage each member who is living the Christian life to practice tithing, or giving 10 percent of their income. This is a biblical principle that goes all the way back to the book of Genesis, when Abram brings a tithe to Melchizedek (see Gen. 14:18–20). Tithing is a visible way of acknowledging that God has authority over every aspect of our lives, including our finances, while also revealing that we believe God is our provider. At the same time, the tithe provides for those who answer the call to serve God on a full-time basis. If every church member tithed regularly, the church would never have a financial shortfall, and the impact of Christianity on this world would increase significantly. At this time only about 4 to 5 percent of churchgoers give a full tithe. Interestingly, 97 percent of those who tithe give more than 10 percent. Those who are generous are very generous, and are supporting the work of the church and Christianity around the world.[4]

When the community of faith works together, society benefits. The community members who can work, do work, and they are not greedy with what they receive. They provide for themselves and for those who are in need and do not grow weary in doing good. We are to be a people who press toward wellness in a spirit of humility.

The call to resist greed is central to the Christian life, reflecting a commitment to humility, justice, and generosity. Instead of having our eyes on our neighbors and their material goods, we are to keep our eyes focused on Jesus. In a world obsessed with wealth and status, the resisting greed is a powerful

---

4. Carey Nieuwhof, "Church Giving Statistics for 2025: Who's Giving, When, and How Much?" n.d., https://careynieuwhof.com/church-giving-statistics/.

testimony to the sufficiency of Christ and the beauty of a life lived in obedience to him.

Questions for Reflection

1. What are examples of economic practices that are shaped by greed? How might these practices trap vulnerable people?

2. What do you think about John Wesley's advice to "gain all you can and save all you can so you can give all you can?"

3. How have you seen the impact of "health and wealth" or "prosperity gospel" preaching?

4. Why is it important to have a strong work ethic?

5. How might a Christian be tempted to gain more wealth or material possessions?

14
ATTITUDES AND ACTIONS THAT DEVALUE OTHERS (¶29.6)

◆ 29.6. We call our people to reject attitudes and actions that undermine the good of people and devalue individuals. All humans are created in the image of God and Christ died for all, therefore every person we encounter merits our highest regard and love. As a people of God, reflecting Christ's love for the world, we reject all forms of racism, ethnic preferences, tribalism, sexism, religious bigotry, classism, exclusionary nationalism, and any other form of prejudice. All of these are contrary to God's love and the mission of Christ.
(Gen. 1:27; Ps. 139:13–14; James 2:1–4; Eph. 2:14–16; Acts 10:34–35)

The concept of human dignity is deeply rooted in our belief that every person is created in the image of God.

Genesis 1:27 (NRSVUE)

So God created humans in his image, in the image of God he created them; male and female he created them.

This truth establishes the sacred worth of every human being regardless of race, gender, nationality, or social status.

Every single person is uniquely created by God to be an instrument of praise to God.

Psalm 139:13-14

For you created my inmost being; you knit me together in my mother's womb.

I praise you because I am fearfully and wonderfully made; your works are wonderful, I know that full well.

Any devaluing of others directly contradicts the very essence of God's creative purpose. It also undermines our ability to follow the command of Jesus Christ to "love one another" (John 13:34). This is not a conditional or selective love but extends to every individual, regardless of perceived differences. Loving others is not optional but a divine mandate.

Prejudice and discrimination undermine the gospel's message of grace and unity. The scriptures also warn us against favoritism.

James 2:1-4

My brothers and sisters, believers in our glorious Lord Jesus Christ must not show favoritism. Suppose a man comes into your meeting wearing a gold ring and fine clothes, and a poor man in filthy old clothes also comes in. If you show special attention to the man wearing fine clothes and say, "Here's a good seat for you," but say to the poor man, "You stand there" or "Sit on the floor by my feet," have you not discriminated among yourselves and become judges with evil thoughts?

When followers of Jesus practice inclusive behavior, they illustrate that all people are equally valuable in God's sight.

Whether a person is the same race, ethnic background, or speaks the same language as we do is irrelevant because we seek to love all people as precious in God's sight. Prejudice in any form contradicts the Christian call to impartial love.

Ephesians 2:14-16

For he himself is our peace, who has made the two groups one and has destroyed the barrier, the dividing wall of hostility, by setting aside in his flesh the law with its commands and regulations. His purpose was to create in himself one new humanity out of the two, thus making peace, and in one body to reconcile both of them to God through the cross, by which he put to death their hostility.

The presence of the Prince of Peace in our lives means we actively engage in bridge building. Chrysostom tells us, "He did not pass the task of reconciliation on to another. He made himself the means of combining one with the other. This produced one wonderful result. He himself was the first instance of this reconciliation, a result greater than all the previous creation."[1] Jesus was the great reconciler, and if we follow his example, then we become agents of reconciliation in this age.

Acts 10:34-35

Then Peter began to speak: "I now realize how true it is that God does not show favoritism but accepts from every nation the one who fears him and does what is right.

To live out the Christian life, we need to examine our personal attitudes. Making time for self-reflection and repen-

---

1. Chrysostom, "Homily on Ephesians 5.2.15."

tance for our biases is essential. Sometimes we are not aware that our actions toward others may be demeaning. It is easy to get wrapped up in our own world and sometimes simply fail to understand someone else's perspective. We may fail to see that others don't receive the same respect or treatment that we receive. When our eyes are opened to see how others are treated, then God can use us to open doors and provide opportunities for others.

Our churches need to foster a spirit of inclusion, becoming welcoming and diverse communities that reflect the breadth of God's kingdom. In this ever-changing world, where people are on the move, migrating from country to country, we have unique opportunities to put these characteristics of Christ into practice. By teaching and modeling equality and respect in the church community, we will pass along this attitude of respect for generations to come.

Questions for Reflection

1. If we truly believed that every individual was a sacred creation of God, how would that belief change the way we live?

2. What are some practical ways we can be inclusive in the church?

3. How can we be intentional about seeing things from others' perspectives?

15
LOYALTIES THAT COMPETE WITH CHRIST'S LORDSHIP (¶29.7)

◆ 29.7. We call our people to resist any loyalty that would compete with Christ's Lordship, which is idolatry. We reject joining any oath-bound societies whether political, secret orders, or guilds that would dilute commitment to Christ and prevent open, transparent communication of primary allegiances. The cost of this refusal can be very real; so, the Christian community must offer support to those who resist.
(Exod. 1:17; Dan. 6:10; Acts 5:29; Rev. 7:14)

The foundation of Christian faith rests on the acknowledgment of Jesus Christ as Lord. In Philippians 2 we read: "Therefore God exalted him to the highest place and gave him the name that is above every name, that at the name of Jesus every knee should bow, in heaven and on earth and under the earth, and every tongue acknowledge that Jesus Christ is Lord, to the glory of God the Father (vv. 9–11)." This confession asserts that Jesus, as Lord, has ultimate authority over every area of life. Therefore, any competing loyalty—whether to ideologies, organizations, or individuals—constitutes idolatry. This is a direct violation of the first of the Ten Commandments, "You shall have no other gods before me" (Exod. 20:3). Total allegiance to Christ is the defining characteristic of Christian discipleship.

Today, many face pressure to become participants in political movements, secret orders, and guilds. One of the more well-known secret orders is Freemasonry. Historically, the Catholic Church and many Protestant denominations have noted the heterodox views of the Masons, which are in direct opposition to our commitment to Christ.

Throughout Scripture, we find examples of those who paid the price to remain loyal to God.

Exodus 1:17

The midwives, however, feared God and did not do what the king of Egypt had told them to do; they let the boys live.

The Jewish midwives feared God more than they feared the government authorities in Egypt. Even at the threat of punishment, these women were faithful and served God. The result was that God could use them and their faithful obedience to save the lives of many. God is constantly seeking followers who are willing to be obedient, even when faced with persecution.

While in exile, Daniel was told to worship the king. He had known the commands of God from childhood, and even the threat of death could not compel him to break God's law. He would never allow another god to receive first place in his life. He didn't even hide his faithfulness.

Daniel 6:10

Now when Daniel learned that the decree had been published, he went home to his upstairs room where the windows opened toward Jerusalem. Three times a day he got down on his knees and prayed, giving thanks to his God, just as he had done before.

As a result of his fidelity to God, Daniel was thrown into the lion's den. God cared for Daniel and closed the mouths of the lions, and his life became a testimony of complete loyalty to God.

After Jesus returned to heaven, the apostles had to wrestle with how they would live. They were tempted by the things of the world, yet this little band of believers chose God over everything else.

Acts 5:29

Peter and the other apostles replied: "We must obey God rather than human beings!"

They began to declare verbally, "Jesus is Lord!" This was radical in an empire that believed Caesar was Lord. Many of the original followers of Jesus would become martyrs for the faith, willing to die rather than submit to any other authority in their lives. During his reign, Nero dipped Christians in tar, lit them on fire, and used them to light his gardens. The pain they suffered was horrific, and seems to be alluded to in the book of Revelation:

Revelation 7:14

I answered, "Sir, you know."

SECTION II

And he said, "These are they who have come out of the great tribulation; they have washed their robes and made them white in the blood of the Lamb."

There is no promise that this obedience will be easy. Even today, some are losing their lives for the faith. The cost of converting to Christianity from Islam or other faiths may be great. Within our church communities, we may discover those who are paying a high price for following Jesus. Believers may encounter discrimination, career setbacks, or strained relationships due to their allegiance to Christ. The early church in Acts 2:42–47 provides us with an example of mutual support, prayer, and communal sharing that helped sustain those who were in need because of their faith.

To maintain Christ's lordship in our everyday lives, we need to regularly evaluate our personal commitments and ensure that no relationship, career, or ideology takes precedence over Christ. Discipleship needs to be prioritized by engaging in Bible study, worship, and service to others to deepen the faith and strengthen resistance to competing influences. We are called to live with integrity, witnessing boldly that we trust in God's ultimate authority and provision. Finally, we must stay rooted in Scripture and prayer.

While the cost of allegiance may be high, the reward is eternal. By relying on God's strength and the support of the Christian community, believers can remain steadfast, proclaiming with confidence, "Jesus Christ is Lord" (Phil. 2:11).

Questions for Reflection

1. What obstacles keep us from truly embracing Jesus as Lord in our lives?

2. What do we encounter in life that is crying out for our time and attention, wanting to supplant the place of Jesus?

3. What are examples of situations today where someone may be tempted to compromise their faith?

4. How can we support those who are experiencing persecution for their faith?

16
CORRUPTION (¶29.8)

◆ 29.8. We call our people to resist corruption in all its forms. All forms of corruption undermine humanity, and create unhealthy divisions in communities and societies. We must resist the temptation to be drawn into corrupt practices such as the use of power to get our own way, manipulate others, engage in bribery, rely on wealth to buy influence, support practices of corruption, and harass or draw others into corruption.
(Lev. 19:11, 13, 15; Luke 3:8, 10–14; Heb. 13:5)

Corruption is a worldwide problem that costs society in political, economic, and environmental ways. The consequences of corruption are most damaging for the financially vulnerable. At the core of corruption is selfishness—the willingness to abuse entrusted power for personal or private gain. Examples of corruption include bribery, inappropriate gifts, double dealing, embezzlement, and defrauding of investors.

Knowing that the love of money would be a temptation for all humanity, God laid out rules regarding the use of money in the law handed down to Moses.

SECTION II

Leviticus 19:11, 13, 15

Do not steal. Do not lie. Do not deceive one another.

Do not defraud or rob your neighbor. Do not hold back the wages of a hired worker overnight.

Do not pervert justice; do not show partiality to the poor or favoritism to the great, but judge your neighbor fairly.

Corrupt attitudes toward money result in the perversion of justice. Throughout Scripture, we discover that justice is a major theme. How we treat others is of great importance to God. It is interesting that Leviticus includes this discussion of day laborers. In many parts of the world, day laborers and immigrants continue to be the most vulnerable and exploited members of society. Even today, making sure a day laborer is paid in a timely manner and has an evening meal is transformational. Jesus suggested that a higher standard, beyond the legal requirement, is expected for his followers (see Matt. 20:1–16). John Wesley saw these behaviors as principles of a life of holiness.

In preparation for the arrival of the Messiah, John the Baptist called people to repentance. Specifically, he preached that this was to result in a change of behavior.

Luke 3:8

Produce fruit in keeping with repentance. And do not begin to say to yourselves, "We have Abraham as our father." For I tell you that out of these stones God can raise up children for Abraham.

There seem to have been three groups present for this declaration—the crowd, the tax collectors, and the soldiers. They asked him specifically what they should do instead.

Corruption

Luke 3:10-14

"What should we do then?" the crowd asked.

John answered, "Anyone who has two shirts should share with the one who has none, and anyone who has food should do the same."

Even tax collectors came to be baptized. "Teacher," they asked, "what should we do?"

"Don't collect any more than you are required to," he told them.

Then some soldiers asked him, "And what should we do?"

He replied, "Don't extort money and don't accuse people falsely—be content with your pay."

Ordinary people were to share generously from what they had been given. This idea of sharing your shirt or undergarment was about giving out of abundance. A person could only wear one shirt at a time, so if you had an extra one, why not share it with someone who didn't have one at all?

The tax collectors were a different issue. These were Jewish people who had become contractors of the Roman Empire, willing to collect taxes from their own people. They were known for their corrupt practices; therefore, to be a tax collector was to abuse one's power among one's own friends and family members, extracting as much as possible so that Rome was paid while allowing the tax collector to become wealthy by keeping the extra income. John told them to stop all corrupt practices and simply collect the legal amount due.

The soldiers comprised the third group, and they were known for extorting money. They would ask for "protection" money, or accuse people of having committed crimes and then offer to "help" keep them from going to prison—for a price.

Repentance meant a radical change in behavior and the end of all corrupt practices.

Ultimately, corruption and greed go hand in hand; they are a condition of the heart. The writer to the Hebrews understood that our attitude toward money had everything to do with our relationship with the Lord.

Hebrews 13:5

Keep your lives free from the love of money and be content with what you have, because God has said, "Never will I leave you; never will I forsake you."

Augustine, a church leader in the fourth and fifth centuries, had this practical advice: "So keep a moderate amount of money for temporal uses; treat it as journey money, with the end in view stated in the text." Notice above all what he put first: "Free from love of money," he says, "put your hand in the purse in such a way that you release your heart from it."[1] Releasing our heart from money is the only way we can be freed from the temptation to greed and corruption. The temptations of this world will always remain, which is why Jesus taught his disciples to pray every day not to be led into temptation. As disciples, we practice self-discipline so we can show God's love and be freed from the love of money.

---

1. Augustine, "Sermon 177.3," J. E. Rotelle, ed. *Works of St. Augustine: A Translation for the Twenty-First Century* (Hyde Park, NY: New City Press, 1995).

Questions for Reflection

1. How can we stay grounded spiritually?

2. Where do you experience corruption in your community?

3. What is the importance of repentance and behavioral change?

CONCLUSION

We are all compelled to continue this journey of grace as we are transformed into Christlike disciples. Just as John the Baptist called people to repentance and a new way of life, so does Jesus. While the world has changed over the last two thousand years, human nature hasn't changed, making the challenge the same in every generation, as different as our circumstances may seem.

We continue to seek the face of Jesus, reflecting him in all we say and do every day of our lives. Our prayer is that you will join us in this journey as we all seek to become more faithful reflections of Jesus to this world.

Questions for Reflection

1. What will you do as a result of this study?

2. What will change in your life moving forward?

www.ingramcontent.com/pod-product-compliance
Lightning Source LLC
LaVergne TN
LVHW051522070426
835507LV00023B/3243